NOT A PLACE TO VISIT

T EDWARD BAK

FLOATING WORLD COMICS
° PORTLAND °

NOT A PLACE TO VISIT

Floating World Comics
400 NW Couch St.
Portland, OR 97209
www.floatingworldcomics.com

First paperback edition May 2020
Printed in China.

ISBN 978-1-942801-76-4

Cover art by T Edward Bak.
Cover design by François Vigneault.

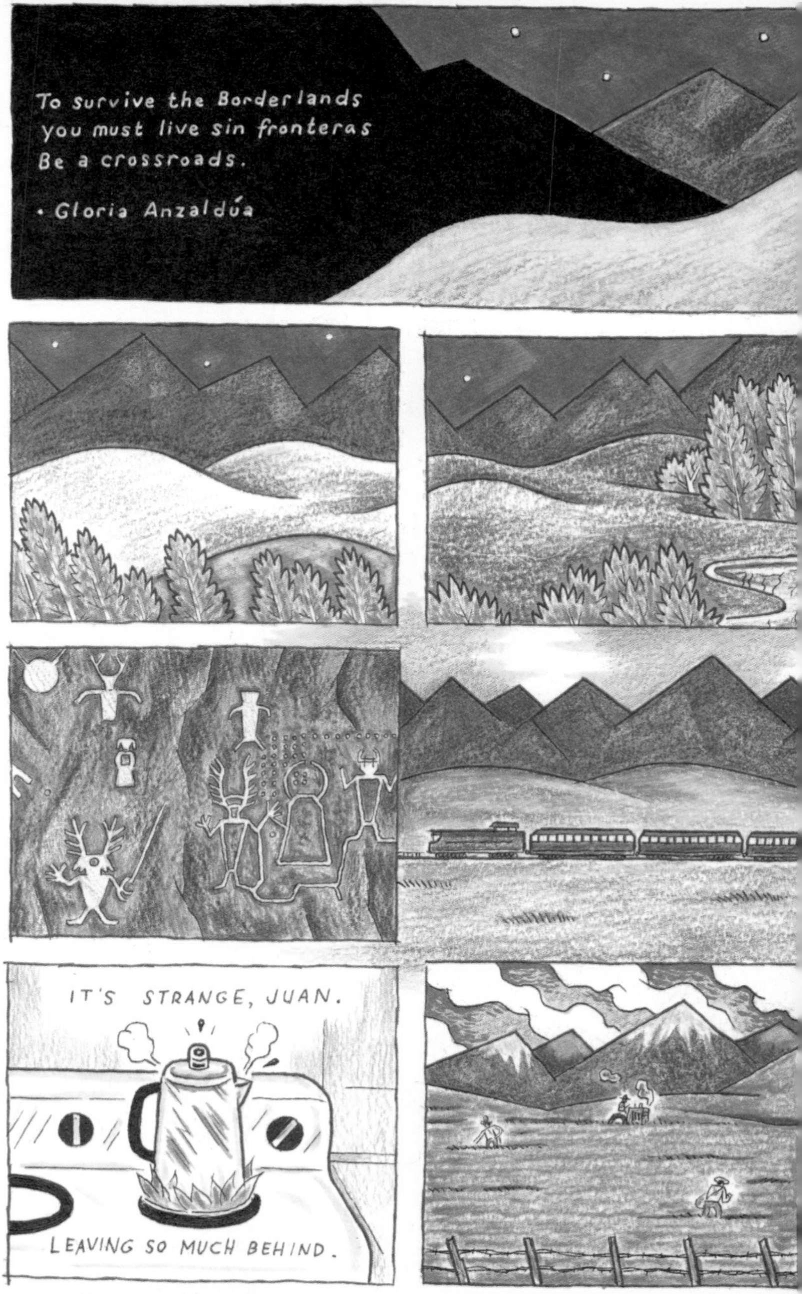
To survive the Borderlands
you must live sin fronteras
Be a crossroads.
• Gloria Anzaldúa
IT'S STRANGE, JUAN.
LEAVING SO MUCH BEHIND.

Scenic fragments of a dream that shadowed the death of my maternal grandfather appose the family history with augmented meaning. I observed passengers in the dream boarding and unboarding a train as it drifted through the prairie along the FRONT RANGE of the COLORADO ROCKY MOUNTAINS. In another panel the image of a rabbit appears; my grandfather was born in the county of CONEJOS — the Spanish word for 'rabbit'.

Despite the temporally distorted vignette a sense of spatial movement across the landscape compels the progress of the narrative.

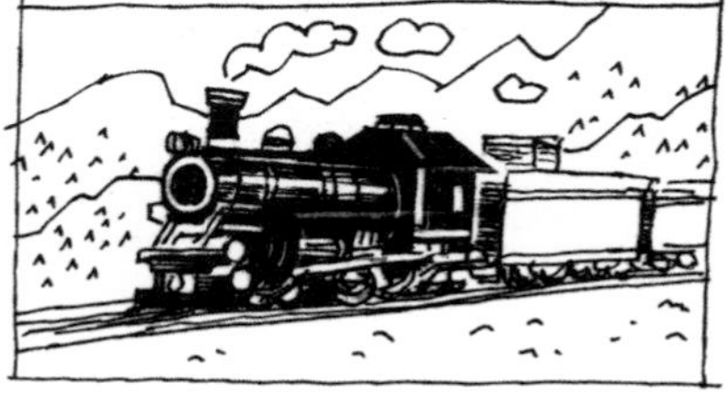

Traveling through the west sometimes feels like going home AWAY from home for me. I wrangle with the significance of a geography that for millenia was circumscribed as sacred space and which now symbolizes mere material function exhibiting the symptoms of its compromised integrity.

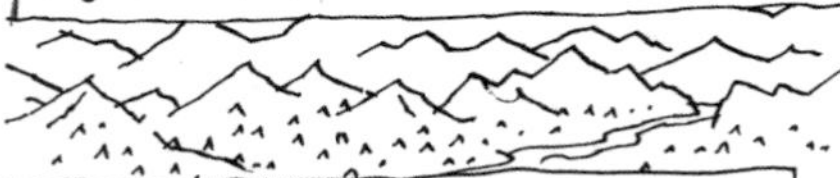

I don't know what it means to be an "American" today. I don't know if I've ever known what it means. Fortunately, the familiarity with my family's continuous presence throughout this part of the west is an ancestral aegis that orients my journey when I am uncertain about the direction of this country or the road under my feet.

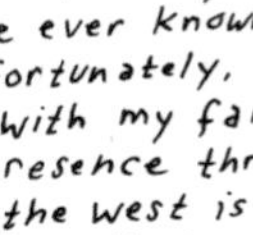
N
W
E
S

REFERENCES

1. Allen, Barbara. SHAPING AND BEING SHAPED BY THE LAND, in THE BIG EMPTY: ESSAYS ON WESTERN LANDSCAPES AS NARRATIVE, ed. LEONARD ENGEL. ALBUQUERQUE: UNIVERSITY OF NEW MEXICO PRESS, 1994.

2. Márquez, Joseph Anthony and Vanessa Anne Márquez. EAST AND WEST of THE SANGRE de CRISTOS PART II: LA FAMILIA MARQUEZ, ed. VANESSA ANNE MÁRQUEZ. Colorado Springs: JAM PRESS, 1994.

3. Simmons, Virginia McConnell. THE SAN LUIS VALLEY: LAND OF THE SIX-ARMED CROSS. Niwot: University Press of Colorado, 1999.

SOMETIMES A PLACE

ORIGINALLY PUBLISHED SEPTEMBER 19, 2016
HIGH COUNTRY NEWS · Frontera Incognita
pp. 36 – 39 · www.hcn.org

"Westerners use stories and story-telling to articulate their sense of connection with the landscape that surrounds them, their sense of place, their regional identity as shaped by place," writes Wyoming folklorist Barbara Allen.[1]

SOMETIMES A PLACE is my first attempt at a form of 'comics essay' designed in an essentially memoir-based format fixing autobiographical narrative at a crossroads of history, geography, culture, and ecology. The entire piece published originally (with the guidance of editor Brian Calvert) in High Country News functions as a juxtaposition of written and illustrated sections.

The comics-oriented nature of this collection provides that only the illustrated narrative is reprinted here.

In the 1850s my mother's ancestors[2] were deeded a land grant by the Mexican government to settle — or, more accurately, to occupy — the San Luis Valley in an area of northern Mexico that would later become Southern Colorado.[3] The illustrated narrative of SOMETIMES A PLACE depicts a continuum of ancestral regional presence leading to my family's most recent northern transit: the move by my maternal grandparents from the San Luis Valley to Denver in 1950.

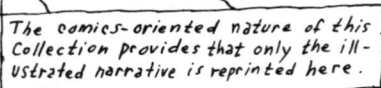

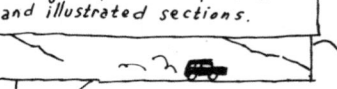

Before I began exploring through comics the intersections of geography and ecology my youthful disregard for history and ancestry provided me with the tools to construct a border against myself — a wall separating me from an inheritance of culture and language I still barely understand.

FOREWORD

In the closing pages of the inimitable *The Snow Leopard* Peter Matthiessen refers to our current era as the time of *Kali Yuga* - the Dark Age. While traveling through western North America my mind is often simultaneously overcome with the beauty of landscapes and with the horrifying truthfulness in the flippant phrase, "Nothing is sacred". Consider for a moment the resignation with which the modern world accepts this bizarre notion. *Nothing is sacred.* Our children grow up embracing and embraced by this conceit while becoming as accustomed to mass extinction as active shooter drills.

The cartoonist capably "writes" in the *gutter* - those spaces in a comic indicated by an actually delineated distinction or the representation of some modal time (and/or 'location') change between "moments" in a scene or between scenes which activate a form of 'storytelling arithmetic' in the mind of the reader. In the interest of expanding narrative possibilities throughout various comics reprinted in this book I have employed the "writing voice" to juxtapose related thematic expressions within and without moments of visual imagery.

I offer an apology in advance to the readers who find themselves confused or vexed by the voice emerging from this series of comics essays. It is not the first time my reach has exceeded my grasp. While creating these works I merely accepted a responsibility for representing an experience informed at crossroads of ecological and cultural phenomena in the western US.

The west is a land scarred by fire, annihilation, glaciation, drought and inundation. It is haunted by theft, torture, kidnaping, rape, scalping, hanging, and slavery. It is cursed by the infestation of Christianity, the Spanish conquista, and the Catholic missions. It is blasphemed by the doctrine of *Manifest Destiny*, by an endless war to claim and re-name its geography, by the betrayal of treaties, and by the preponderance of an enemy to concoct through genocide a specious sovereign history. Was Matthiessen correct? Do humans just have bad timing? Or can we choose to evolve?

I created these comics because I believe human beings value their stories enough to preserve them. Like all of us our stories deserve a place to live and to grow, to be seen and respected and appreciated. Where each one is sacred.

T E Bak

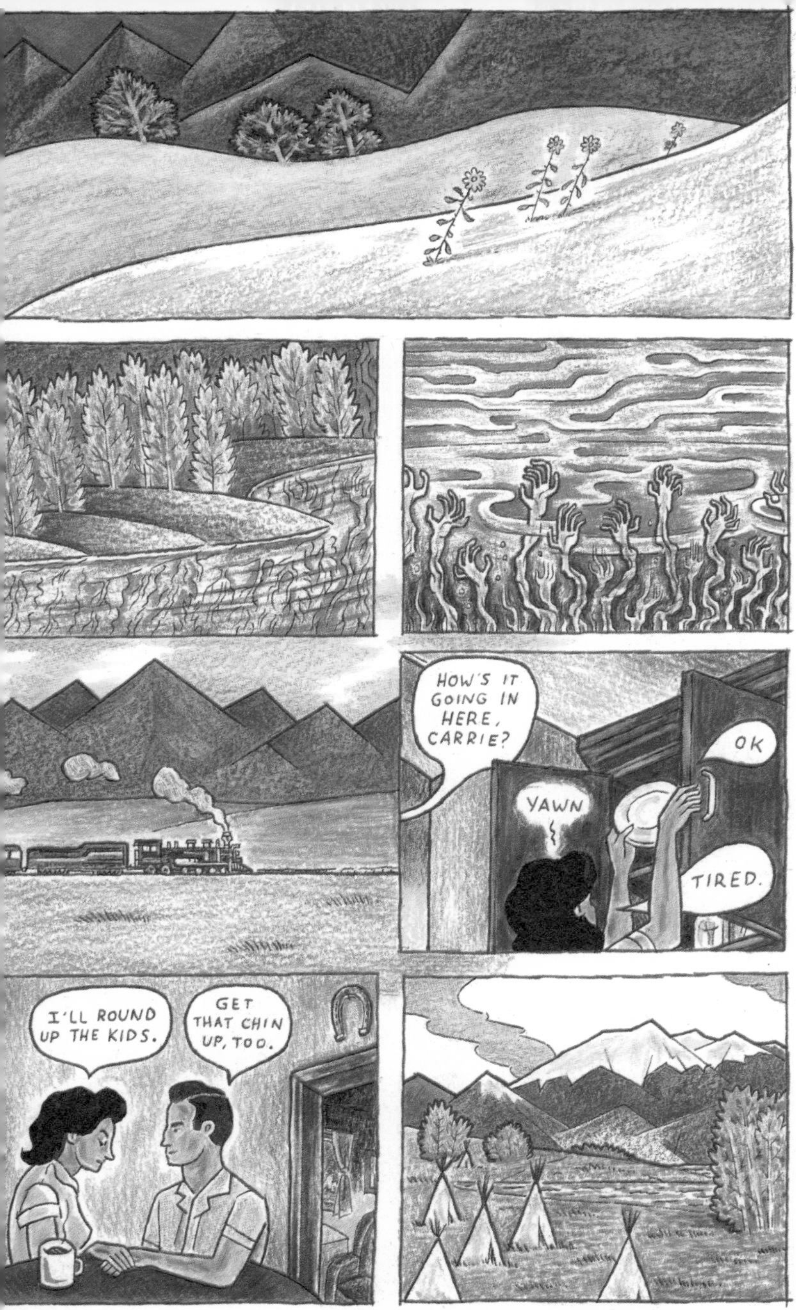
HOW'S IT GOING IN HERE, CARRIE?
OK
YAWN
TIRED.
I'LL ROUND UP THE KIDS.
GET THAT CHIN UP, TOO.

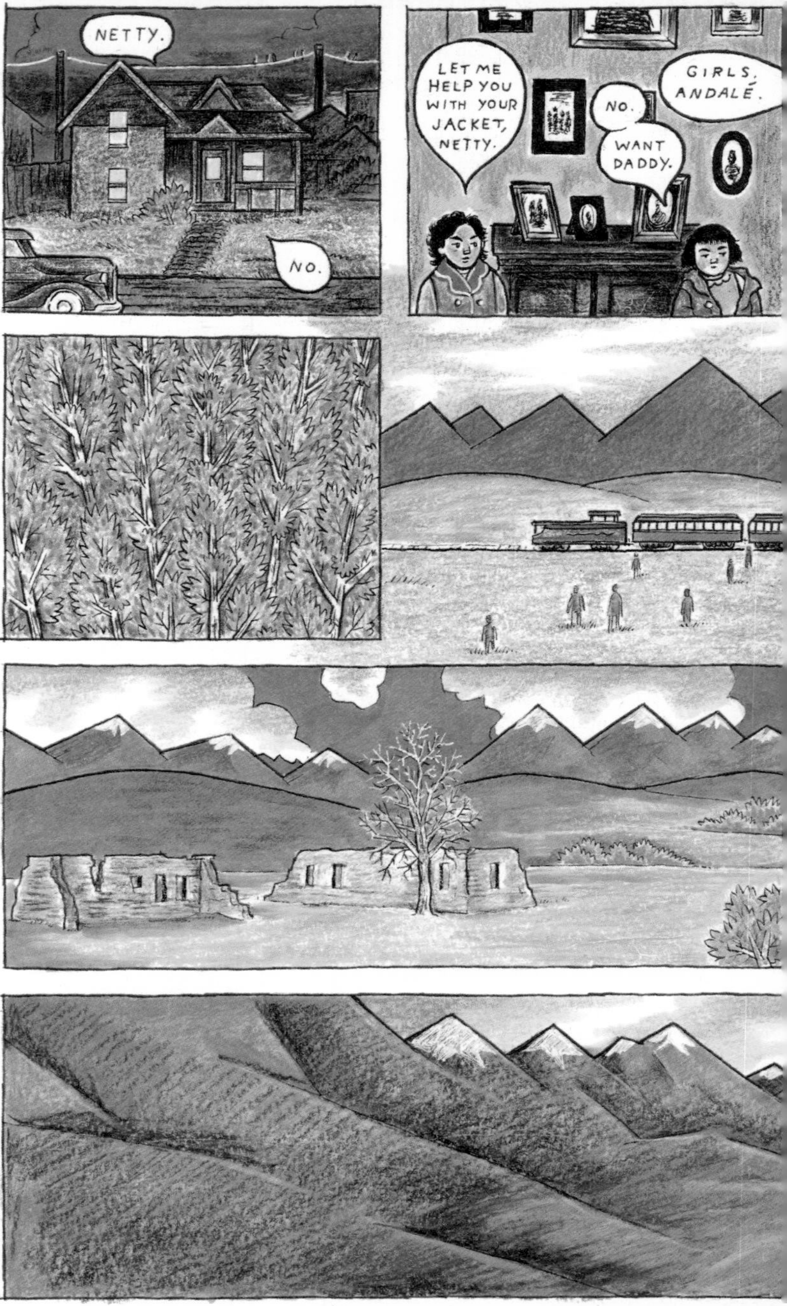
NETTY.
NO.
LET ME HELP YOU WITH YOUR JACKET, NETTY.
NO.
WANT DADDY.
GIRLS. ANDALÉ.

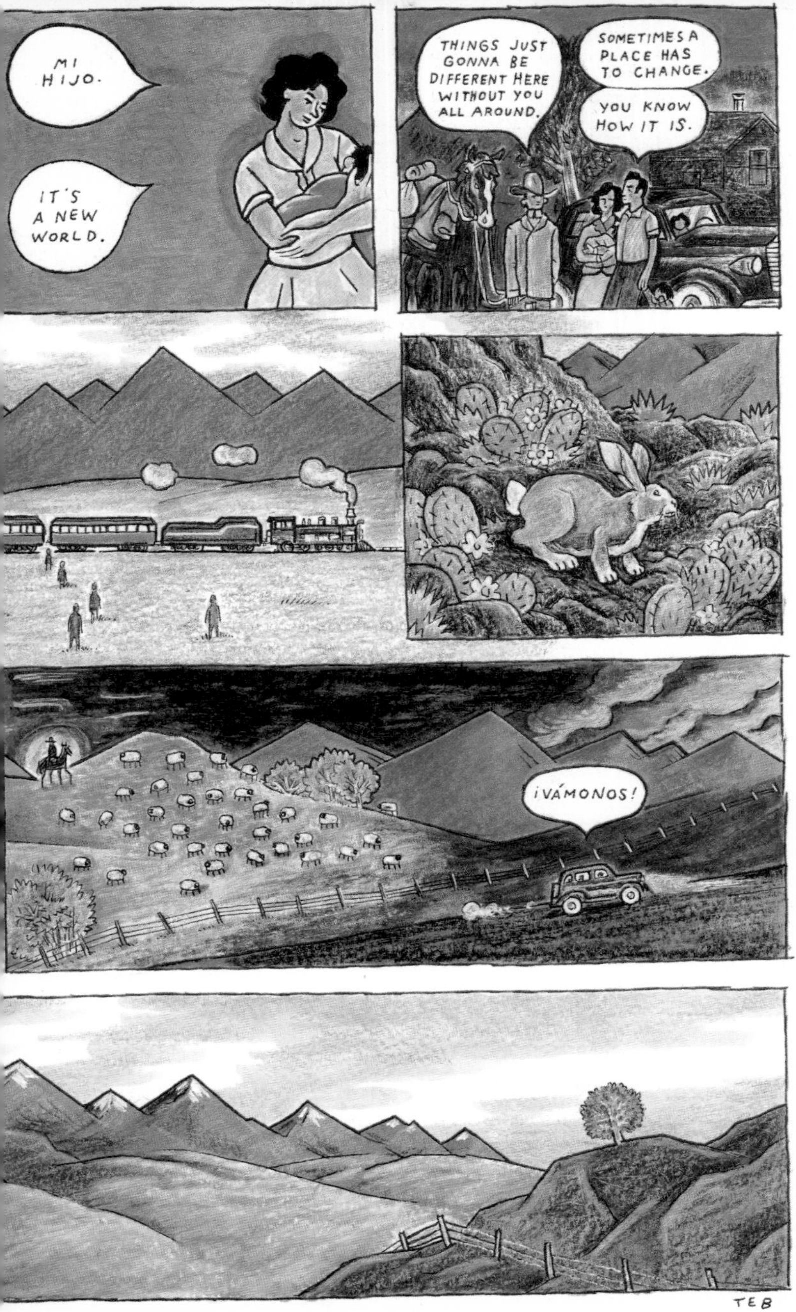
MI HIJO.
IT'S A NEW WORLD.
THINGS JUST GONNA BE DIFFERENT HERE WITHOUT YOU ALL AROUND.
SOMETIMES A PLACE HAS TO CHANGE.
YOU KNOW HOW IT IS.
¡VÁMONOS!
TEB

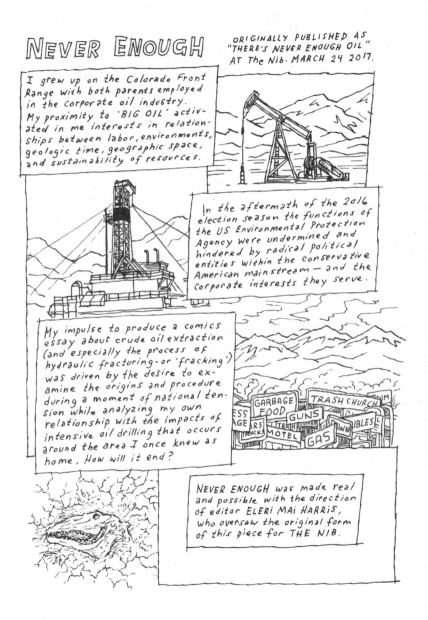

NEVER ENOUGH

ORIGINALLY PUBLISHED AS "THERE'S NEVER ENOUGH OIL" AT The Nib. MARCH 24 2017.

I grew up on the Colorado Front Range with both parents employed in the corporate oil industry. My proximity to 'BIG OIL' activated in me interests in relationships between labor, environments, geologic time, geographic space, and sustainability of resources.

In the aftermath of the 2016 election season the functions of the US Environmental Protection Agency were undermined and hindered by radical political entities within the conservative American mainstream — and the corporate interests they serve.

My impulse to produce a comics essay about crude oil extraction (and especially the process of hydraulic fracturing- or 'fracking') was driven by the desire to examine the origins and procedure during a moment of national tension while analyzing my own relationship with the impacts of intensive oil drilling that occurs around the area I once knew as home. How will it end?

GARBAGE FOOD TRASH CHURCH GUNS MOTEL GAS

NEVER ENOUGH was made real and possible with the direction of editor ELERI MAI HARRIS, who oversaw the original form of this piece for THE NIB.

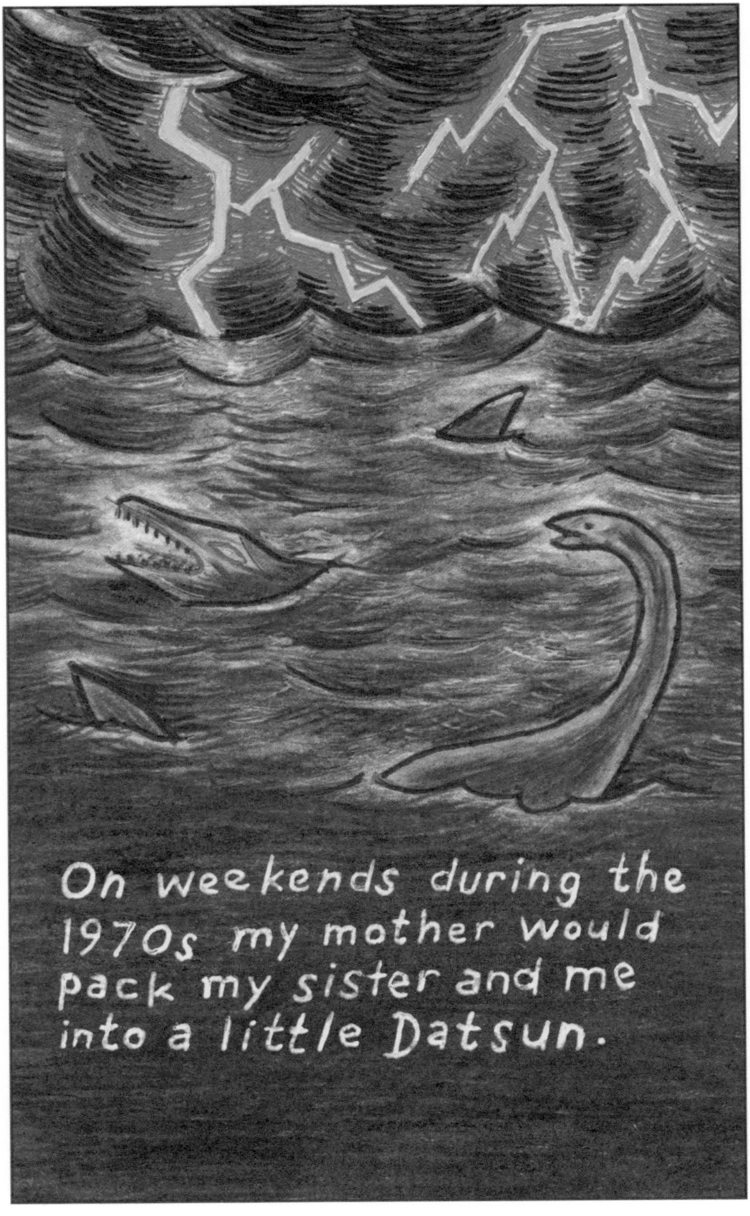
On weekends during the 1970s my mother would pack my sister and me into a little Datsun.

A dozen highway exits
West of Denver we would
climb down to our favorite

picnic spot beside a
mountain stream tumbling
beneath the blue spruce and
bristlecone pines.

On our way out of town
we stopped for fuel. I
still marvel at the ingenuity
of the ubiquitous Sinclair
station sign — a benign
association of petroleum
energy with nature —

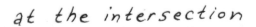

at the intersection

of convenience and mobility.

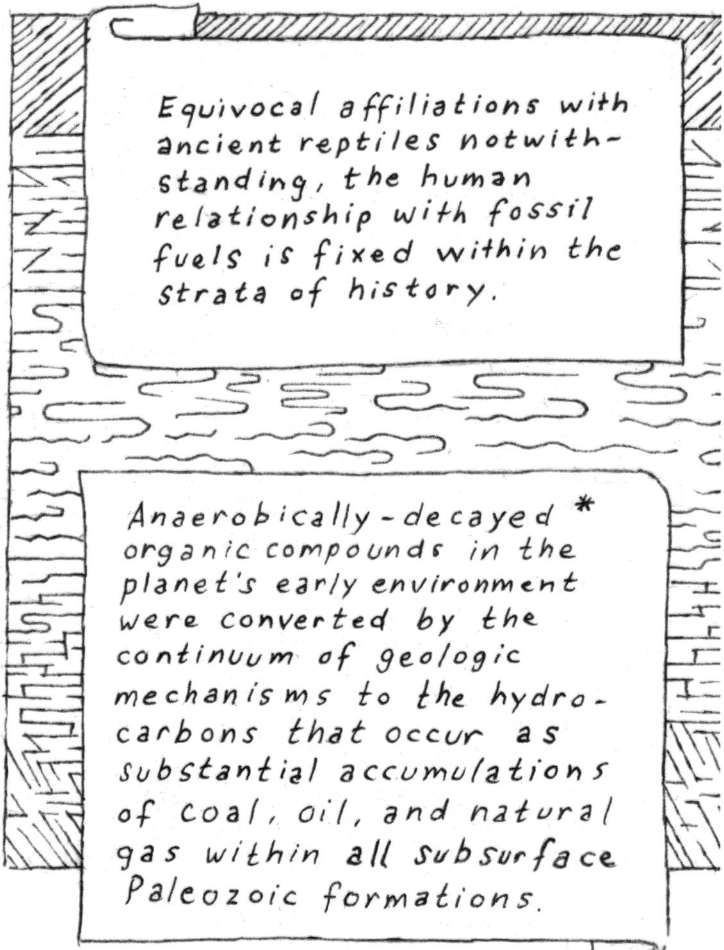
Equivocal affiliations with ancient reptiles notwithstanding, the human relationship with fossil fuels is fixed within the strata of history.
Anaerobically-decayed * organic compounds in the planet's early environment were converted by the continuum of geologic mechanisms to the hydrocarbons that occur as substantial accumulations of coal, oil, and natural gas within all subsurface Paleozoic formations.

* decomposition in the absence of oxygen

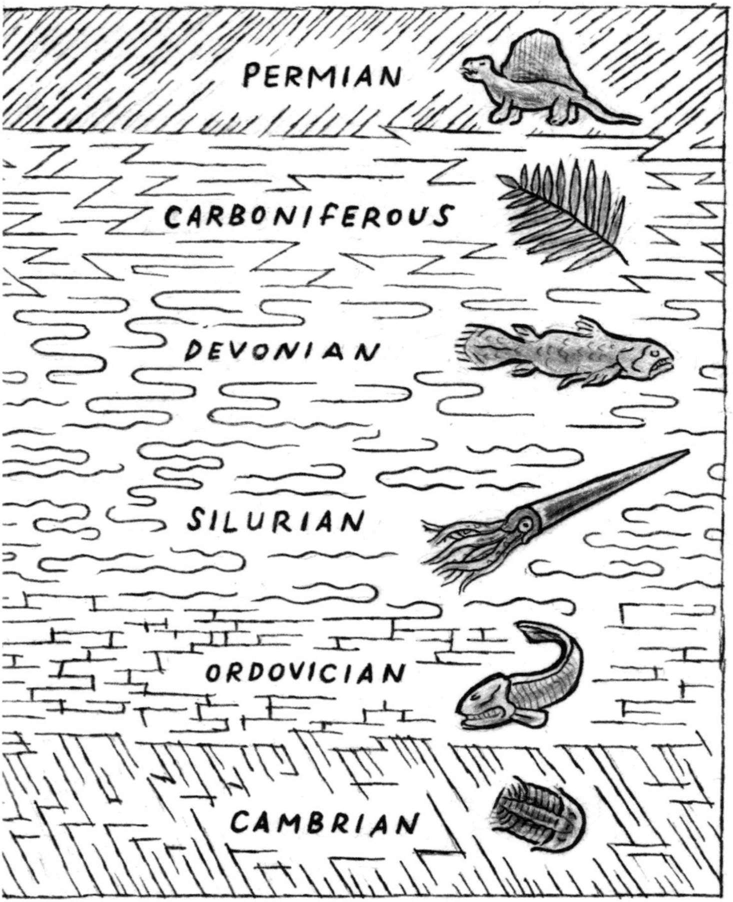
PERMIAN
CARBONIFEROUS
DEVONIAN
SILURIAN
ORDOVICIAN
CAMBRIAN

An estimated 2 billion barrels of retrievable oil is contained in Colorado's Niobrara Shale.

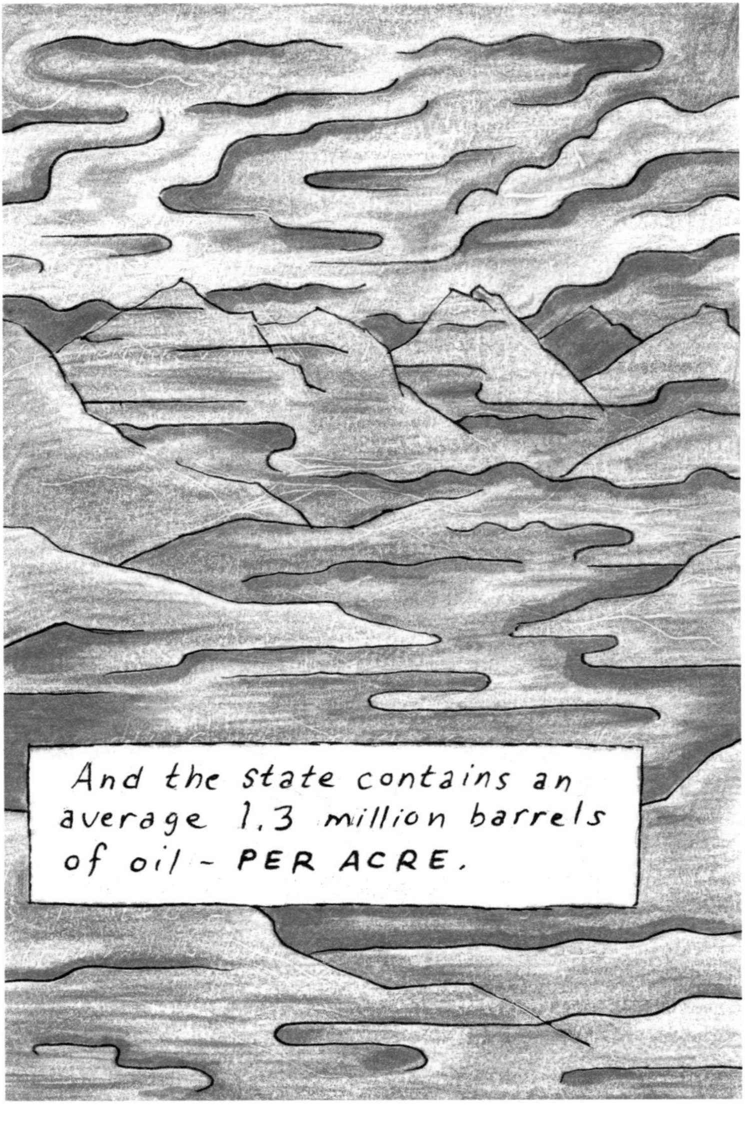
And the state contains an average 1.3 million barrels of oil - PER ACRE.

The modern history of Colorado's fossil fuel usage originates with the state's indigenous peoples.

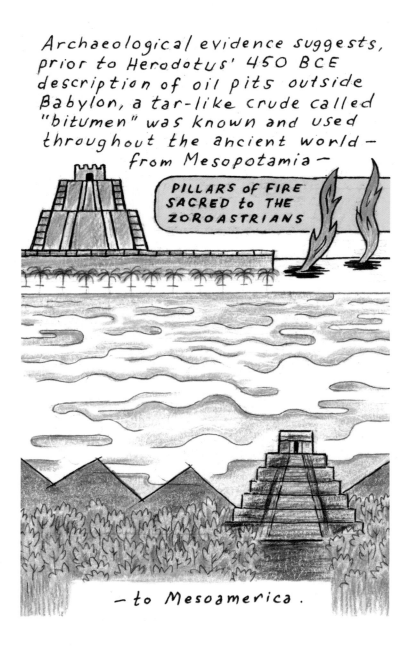

Archaeological evidence suggests, prior to Herodotus' 450 BCE description of oil pits outside Babylon, a tar-like crude called "bitumen" was known and used throughout the ancient world— from Mesopotamia—

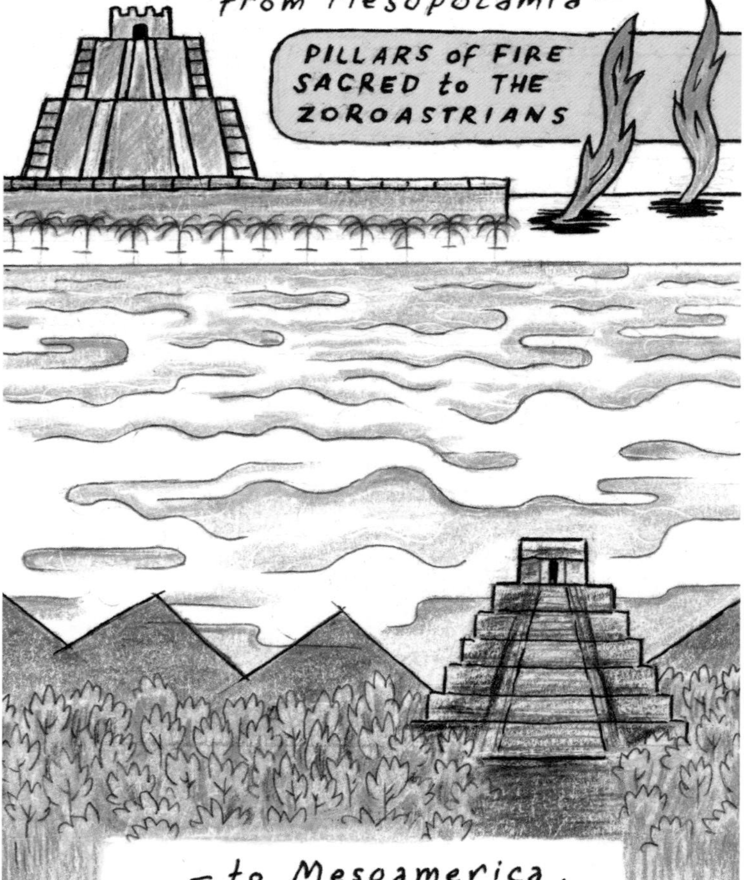
PILLARS OF FIRE SACRED to THE ZOROASTRIANS
—to Mesoamerica.

In the 4th century CE, a percussive drilling method used by Chinese salt miners was developed in Sichuan province.

Fastened with a plank and "see-sawed" by one or two operators, the bamboo drill "kicked down" to tap brine aquifers for groundwater, which was evaporated by a heat source until only salt remained.

This "kicking-down" method became the prototype for the apparatus design now internationally synonymous with oil production: the derrick.

Meanwhile, the Utes harvested crude from oil "seeps" in Colorado for warpaint, waterproofing homes, and sealing woven baskets.

In 1881, Colorado's first oil well was drilled outside CAÑON CITY at what became the oldest producing oilfield in the US — the Denver Basin's Florence field.

My mother worked in the oil and gas industry for 40 years, primarily as a 'landman', beginning with a job analyzing leases for

a small, Denver-based outfit,
when she met and married my
stepfather. Petroleum gave
us a comfortable middle-class
lifestyle; in the summer we
visited the state parks and we
skied the Rockies in winter.

But I grew up oblivious to
the role the petroleum
industry played in the
environment, the global
economy, and the political
landscape of the west.

For a couple of weeks one
summer I visited a well-site
with my step-father, a mud-
logger whose job was analyzing shale samples.
The drilling location was a
hot, deafening belch of iron,
smoke and mud swollen around

a dusty, crusty bruise
of calloused prairie
in rural Colorado.

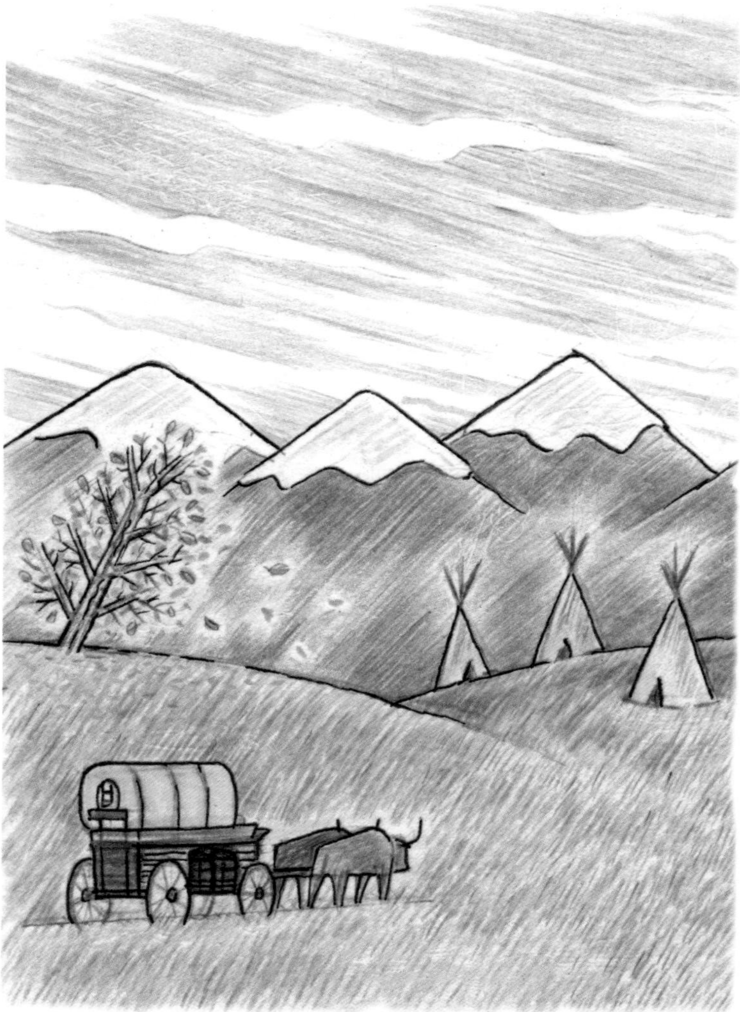

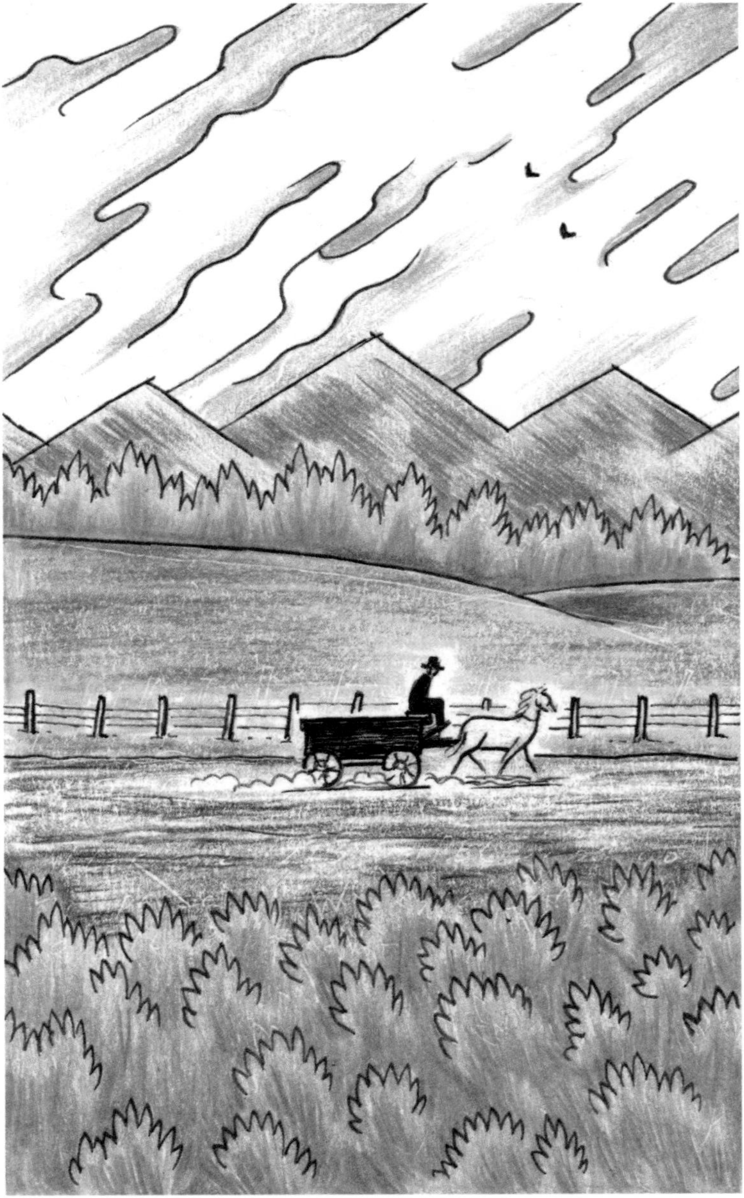

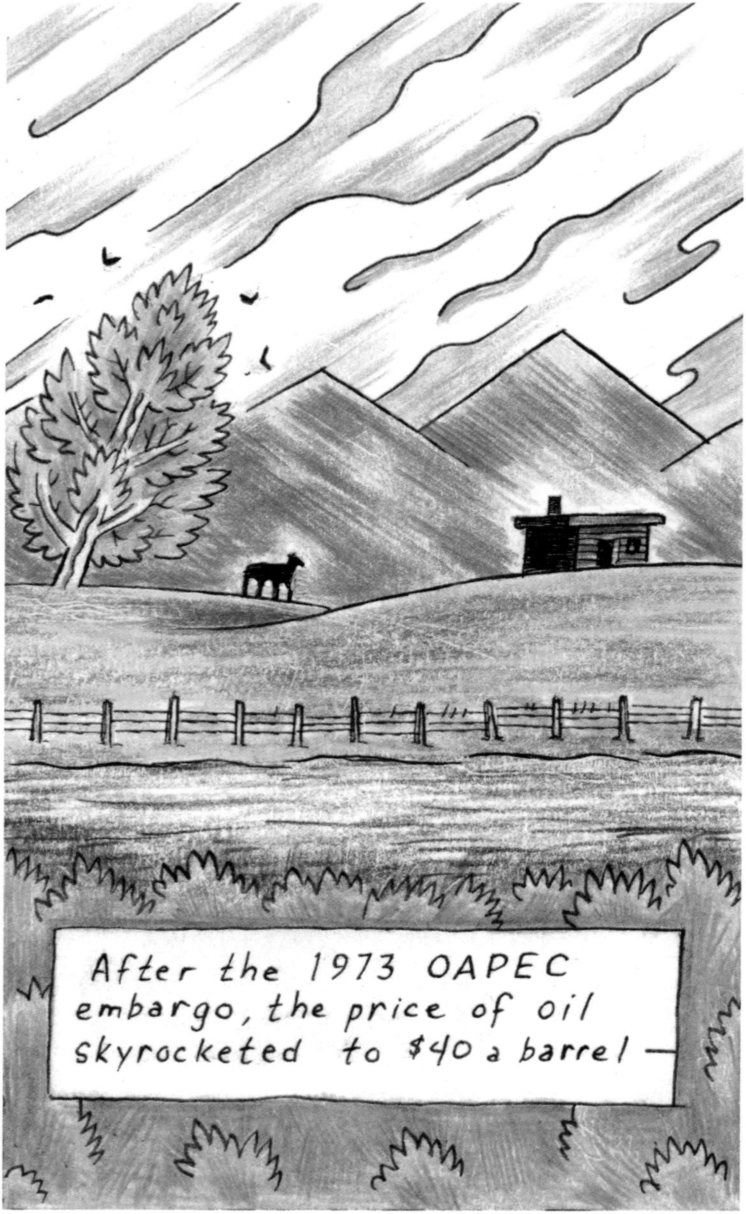
After the 1973 OAPEC embargo, the price of oil skyrocketed to $40 a barrel —

before dropping again in 1982
due to improvements in car
fuel efficiency and a global
oil surplus.

By the 1990s the oil and gas
industry recovered with
higher demand; between 1999
and 2014, production growth
rates for Colorado's oil and
gas increased by 476% and
200%, respectively.

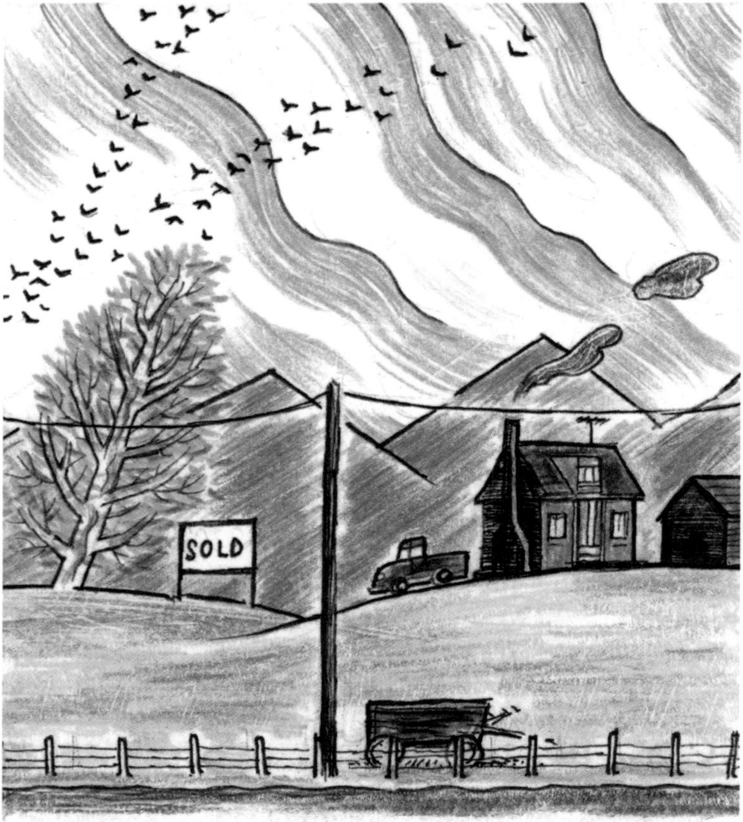
SOLD

But traditional drilling was not driving the rebound.

That distinction belongs to the method of resource extraction known as hydraulic fracturing—or, "fracking".

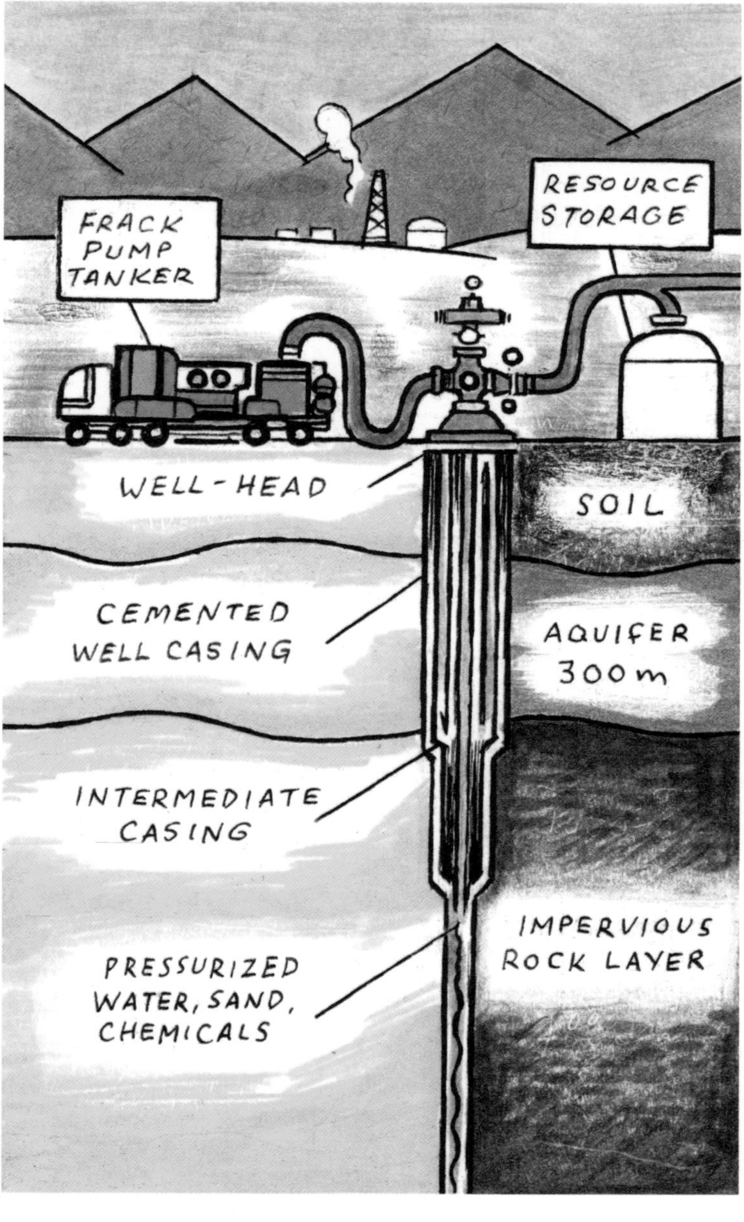
FRACK PUMP TANKER
RESOURCE STORAGE
WELL-HEAD
SOIL
CEMENTED WELL CASING
AQUIFER 300m
INTERMEDIATE CASING
IMPERVIOUS ROCK LAYER
PRESSURIZED WATER, SAND, CHEMICALS

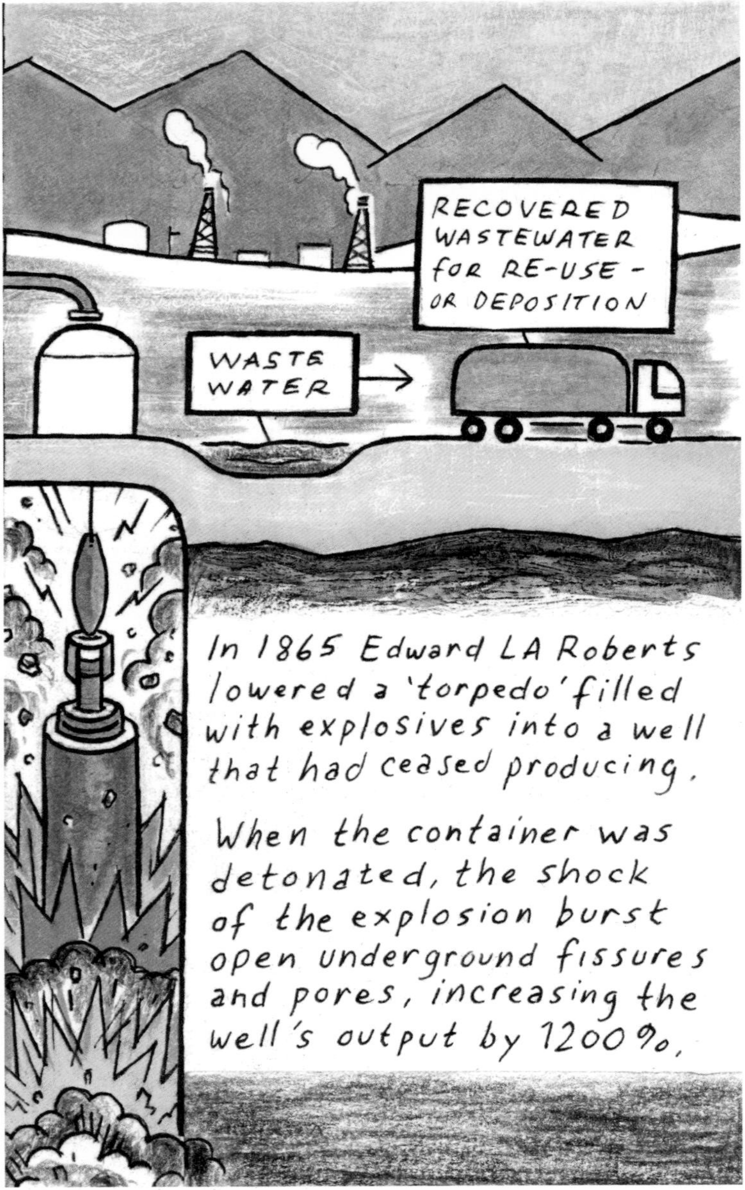
RECOVERED WASTEWATER FOR RE-USE - OR DEPOSITION
WASTE WATER
In 1865 Edward LA Roberts lowered a 'torpedo' filled with explosives into a well that had ceased producing.
When the container was detonated, the shock of the explosion burst open underground fissures and pores, increasing the well's output by 1200%.

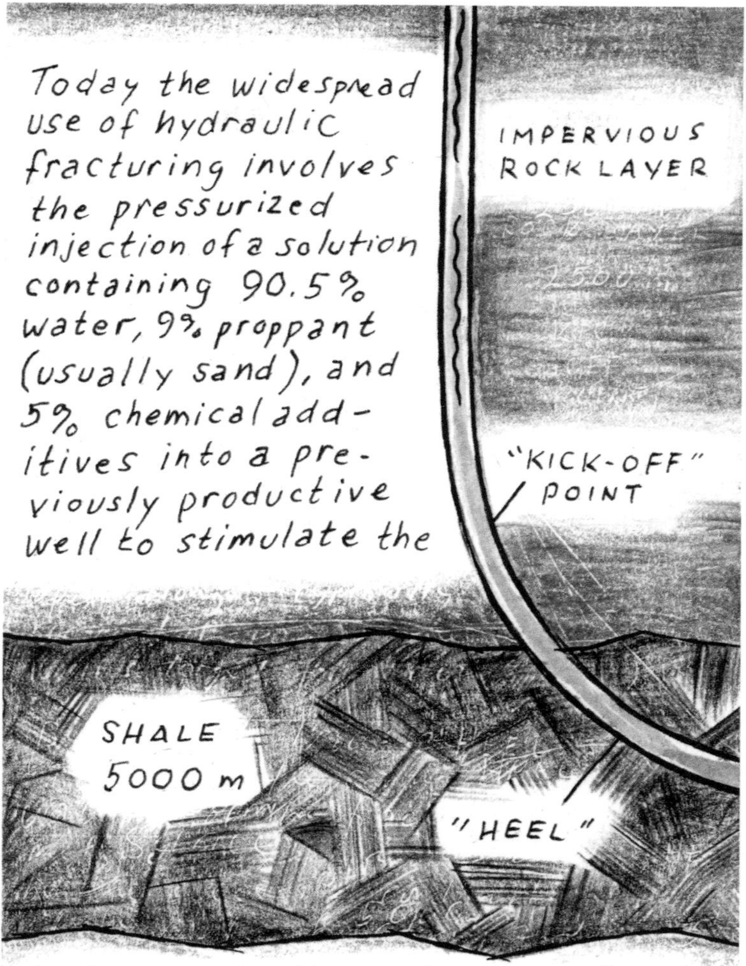
Today the widespread use of hydraulic fracturing involves the pressurized injection of a solution containing 90.5% water, 9% proppant (usually sand), and 5% chemical additives into a previously productive well to stimulate the
IMPERVIOUS ROCK LAYER
"KICK-OFF" POINT
SHALE 5000 m
"HEEL"
release of oil and/or gas from .508 cm fissures fractured open along a typically horizontal span of the well's target formation.

By the late 1980s and early 1990s the commercial viability of the fracking method had been demonstrated by the successful combination of hydraulic fracturing and horizontal drilling of the Barnett Shale in north Texas.

PIPE IS PUNCTURED AND SUCCEEDING FRACTURES BRACED OPEN BY INJECTED SAND RELEASE OIL OR GAS FROM SHALE FOR SURFACE EXTRACTION.

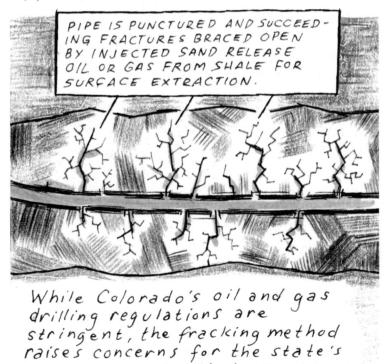

While Colorado's oil and gas drilling regulations are stringent, the fracking method raises concerns for the state's residents nonetheless.

Everyday millions of gallons of freshwater are used and contaminated in fracking operations. A variety of pollutants—including volatile organic compounds and methane—have been released

during the extraction, transportation, or distribution of oil and/or natural gas,

And the emission of known carcinogens has been traced to fracking activity.

Meanwhile, the hydraulic fracturing procedure is implicated as a direct cause of earthquakes in western CANADA

"Most recent cases of induced seismicity are highly correlated in time and space with hydraulic fracturing"

Fracking has also come under fire in Oklahoma, with evidence —

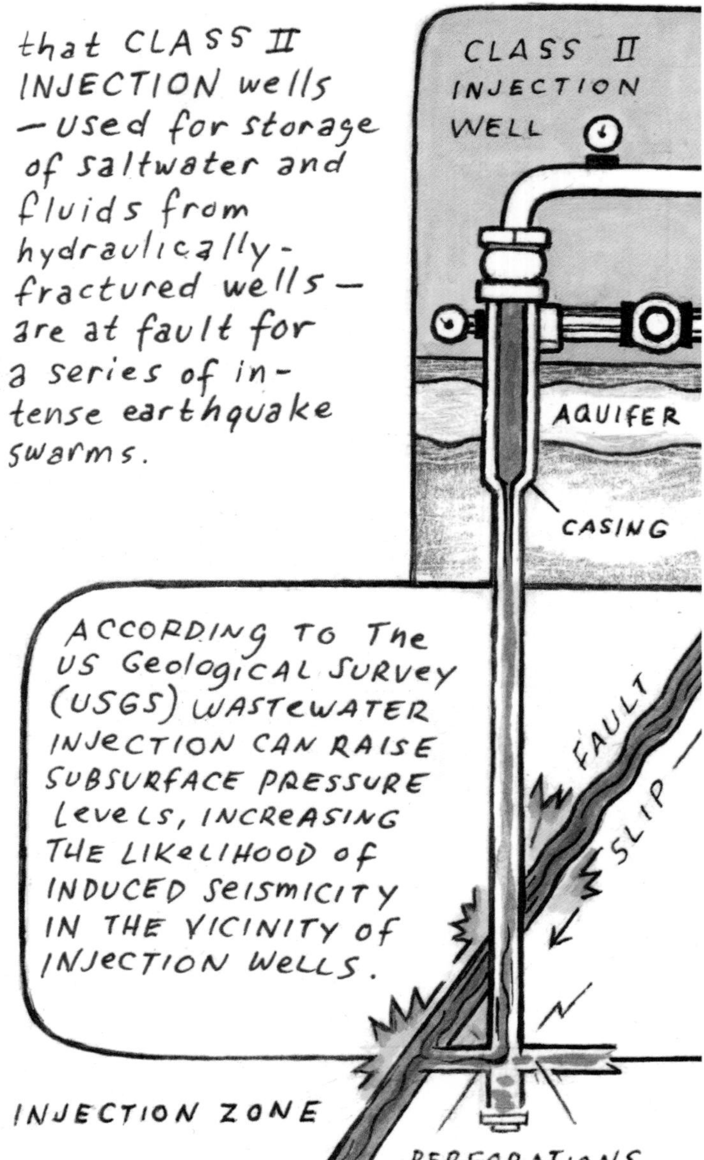
that CLASS II INJECTION wells —used for storage of saltwater and fluids from hydraulically-fractured wells—are at fault for a series of intense earthquake swarms.
CLASS II INJECTION WELL
AQUIFER
CASING
ACCORDING TO THE US GEOLOGICAL SURVEY (USGS) WASTEWATER INJECTION CAN RAISE SUBSURFACE PRESSURE LEVELS, INCREASING THE LIKELIHOOD OF INDUCED SEISMICITY IN THE VICINITY OF INJECTION WELLS.
FAULT
SLIP
INJECTION ZONE
PERFORATIONS

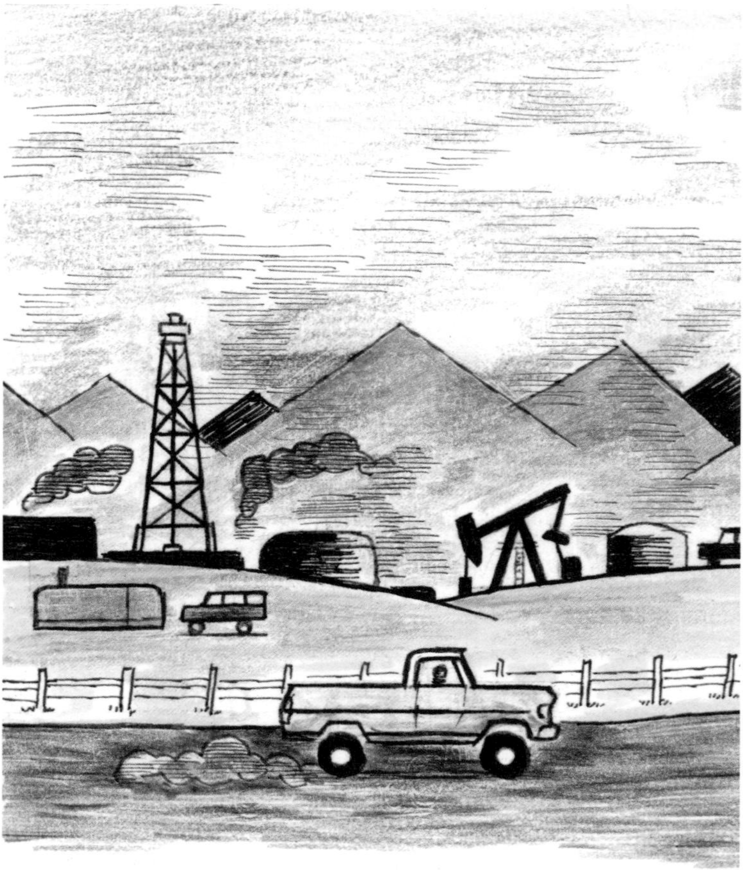

Meanwhile, millions of dollars are invested in the development and engineering of fracking projects, which increase the feasibility of extracting previously inaccessible oil and gas reserves.

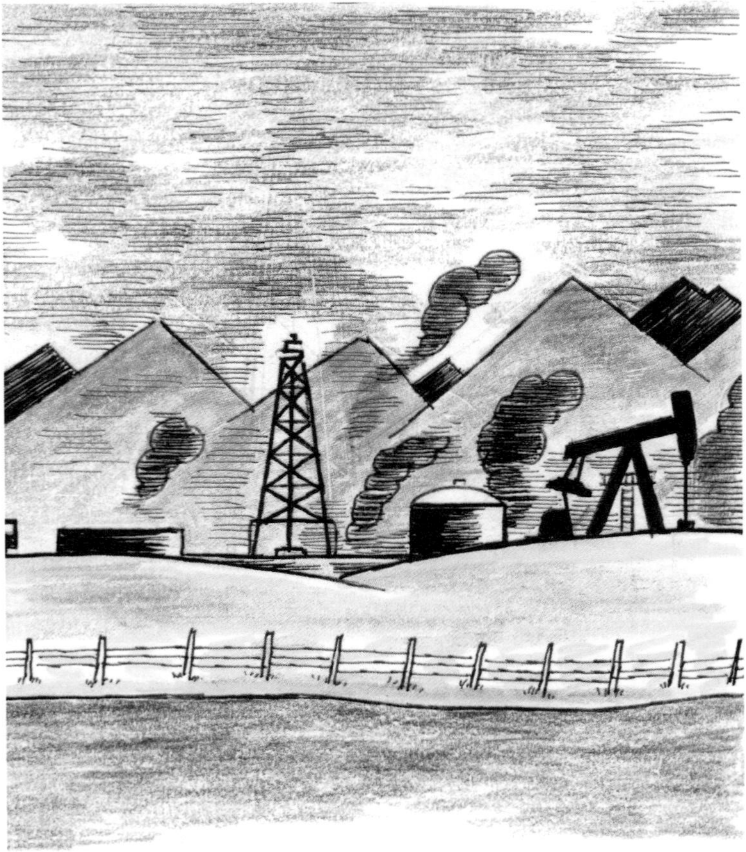

In 2014 the total economic impact of the oil and gas industry in Colorado was $317 billion, directly and indirectly supporting 102,700 jobs statewide.

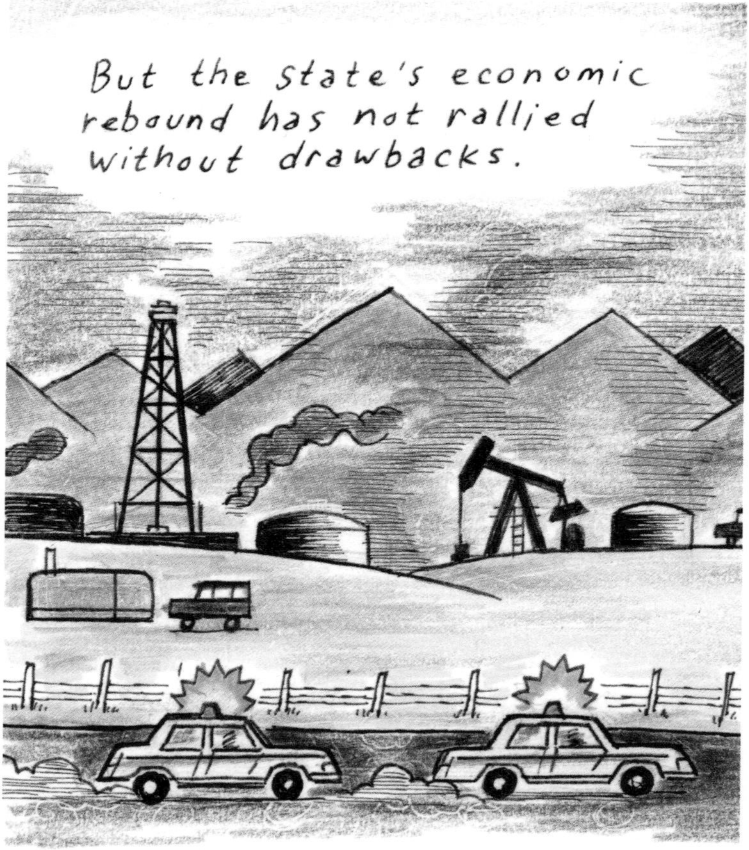
But the state's economic rebound has not rallied without drawbacks.

Large-scale fracking booms frequently occur in rural communities where housing and municipal resources are easily strained, leading to increased crime rates, especially incidents of domestic violence and substance abuse.

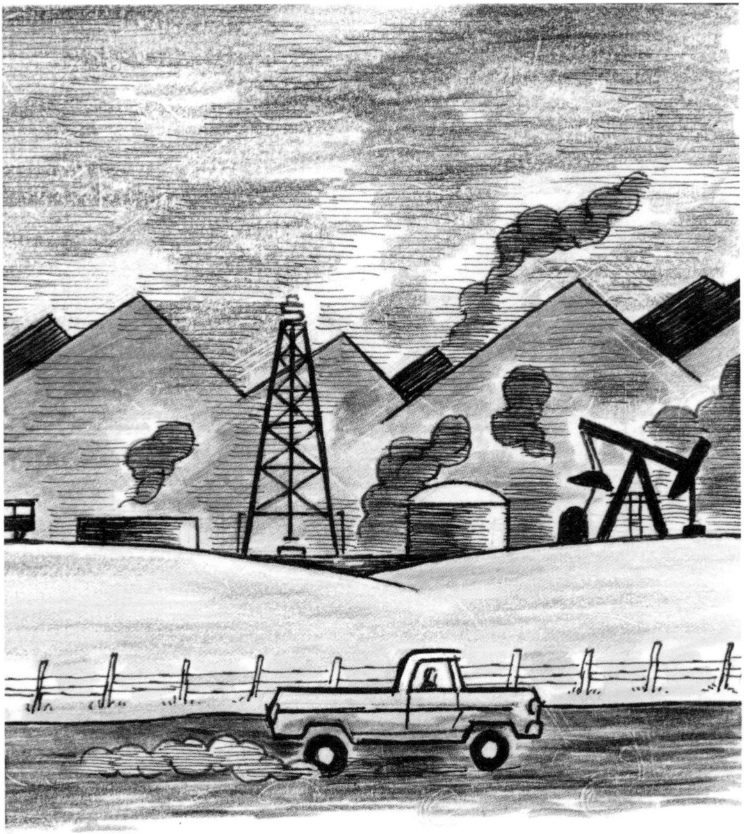

While experiencing a recent boost in oil and gas production, Garfield county hired 15 new police officers to handle the synchronous spike in local crime.

There was a vast prairie east of the development where my parents purchased a new home north of Denver in 1980.

When the sallow days of winter compelled me outdoors I found myself following animal tracks

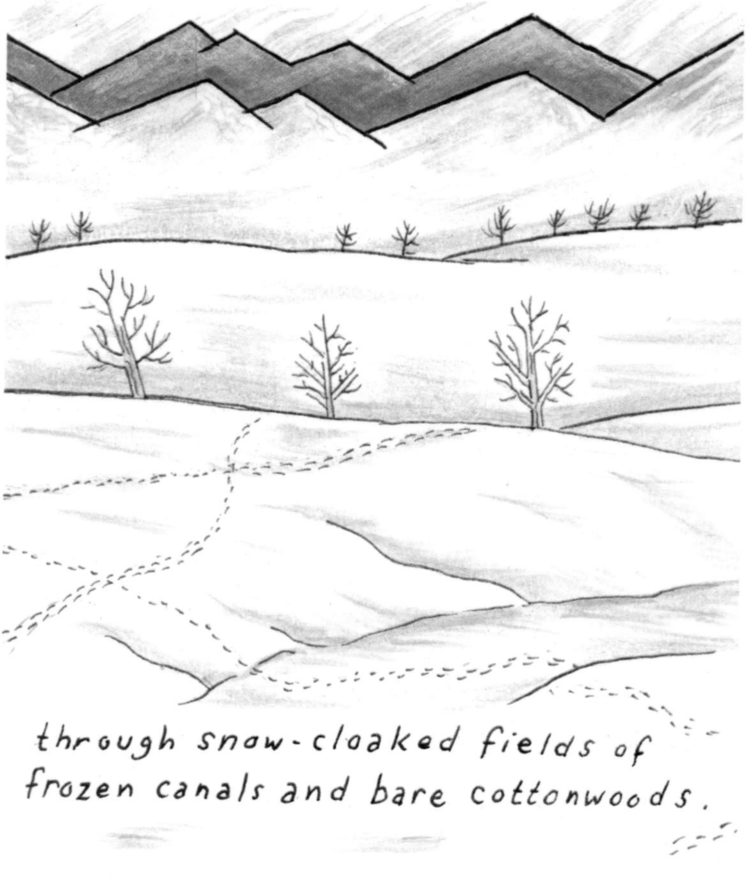

through snow-cloaked fields of frozen canals and bare cottonwoods.

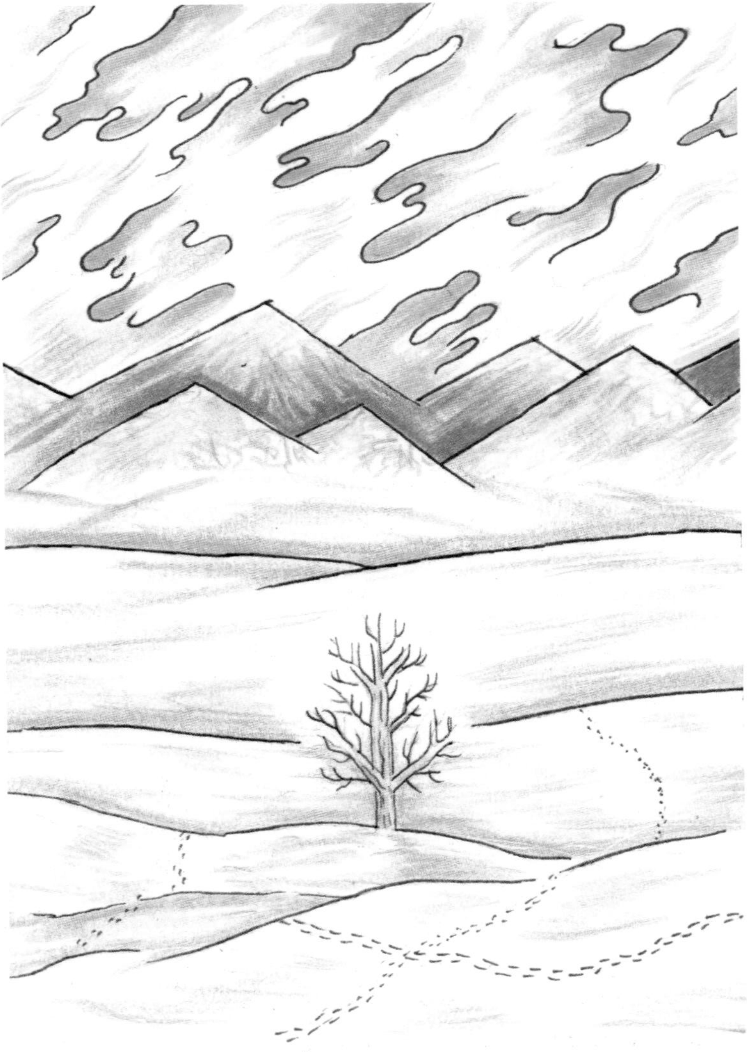

Pheasant, fox, prairie dog,
deer, coyote, quail, hare.

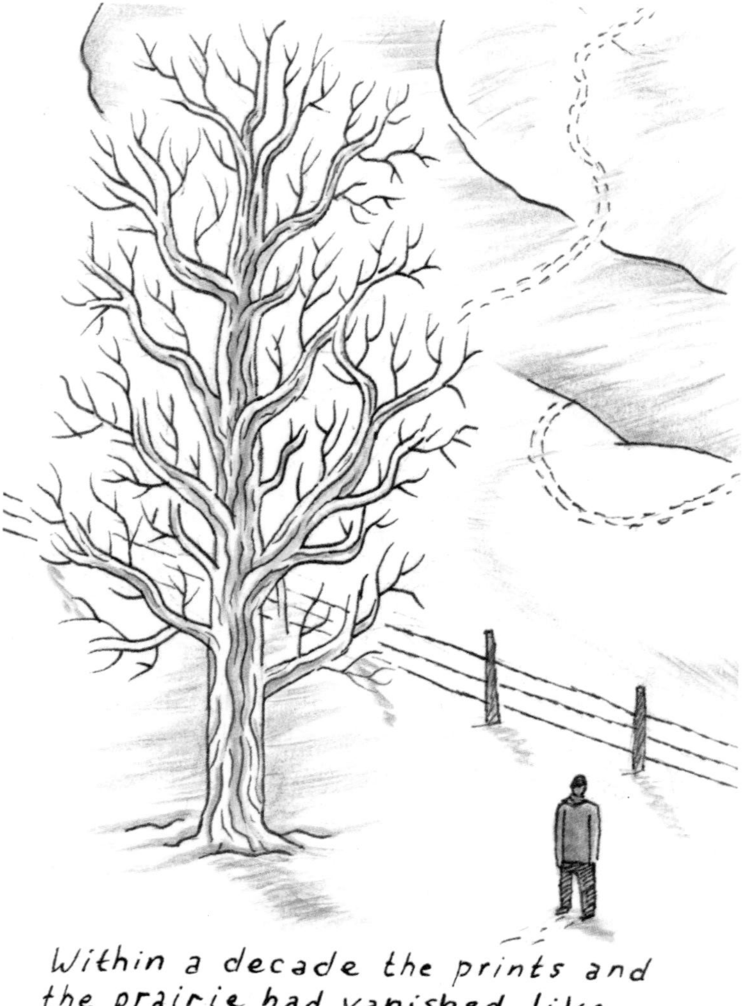

Within a decade the prints and the prairie had vanished like snowmelt in spring.
The house was sold, my parents divorced and today the terrain

is a cluttered bedlam of snarled traffic and fast food strip mall parking lots. Gas stations.

Sometimes I come home to revisit that landscape hoping the violence of its mutation has somehow been redacted.

In the distance there are always more oilfields.

Always more, more, more.

VOICES OF CELILO FALLS / NOT A PLACE TO VISIT

VOICES of CELILO FALLS
ORIGINALLY PUBLISHED IN
OREGON HISTORY COMICS, 2010.

NOT A PLACE TO VISIT ORIGINALLY
PUBLISHED ONLINE AT POPULA -
AUGUST 27, 2018. popula.com

SARAH MIRK and I collaborated on VOICES of CELILO FALLS for the OREGON HISTORY COMICS series. published in 2010; Sarah was the series editor and composed the essential text for this comic while I developed the visual/comics narrative. The work is my first collaboration with another artist. Fortunately, Sarah is as ingenious and inventive as she is receptive, and working with her was a genuine privilege.

NOT A PLACE TO VISIT was guided by the deft editorial hand of Trevor Alixopulos for POPULA. The work serves as a kind of follow-up/companion piece to VOICES of CELILO FALLS; between the publication of the two comics, my interest in ecology, settlement history, traditional indigenous American culture, and traditional ecological knowledge evolved.

I have worked in a handful of positions aboard small tour ships and recognize the value of exploring the historical confluence of labor and class with natural science in economies of regional resource exploitation (i.e., indigenous salmon cultures and salmon fisheries; European-origin settlement; the Columbia River dam system; old-growth timber industry and the tourism industry) which transformed cultures and habitats throughout the PACIFIC NORTHWEST.

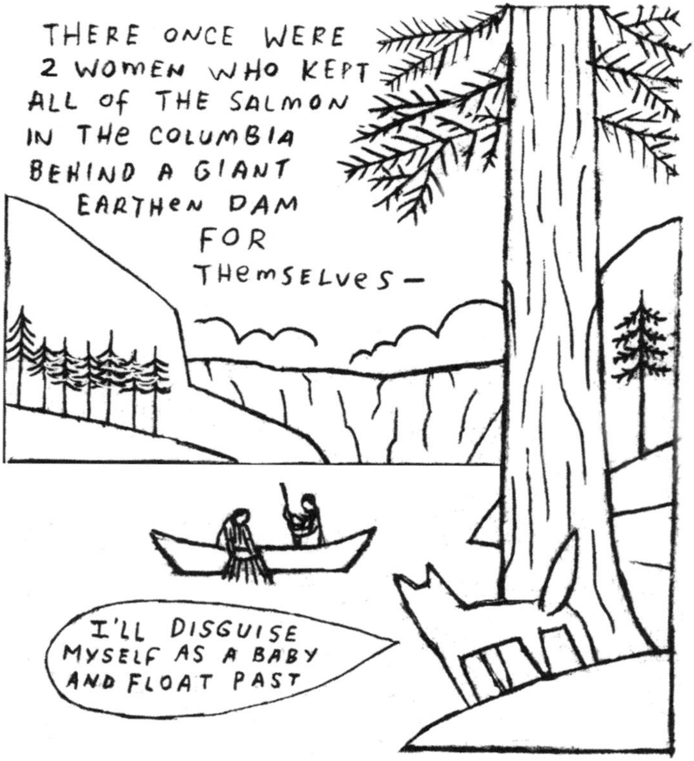
THERE ONCE WERE 2 WOMEN WHO KEPT ALL OF THE SALMON IN THE COLUMBIA BEHIND A GIANT EARTHEN DAM FOR THEMSELVES—
I'LL DISGUISE MYSELF AS A BABY AND FLOAT PAST

BUT COYOTE WAS CLEVER

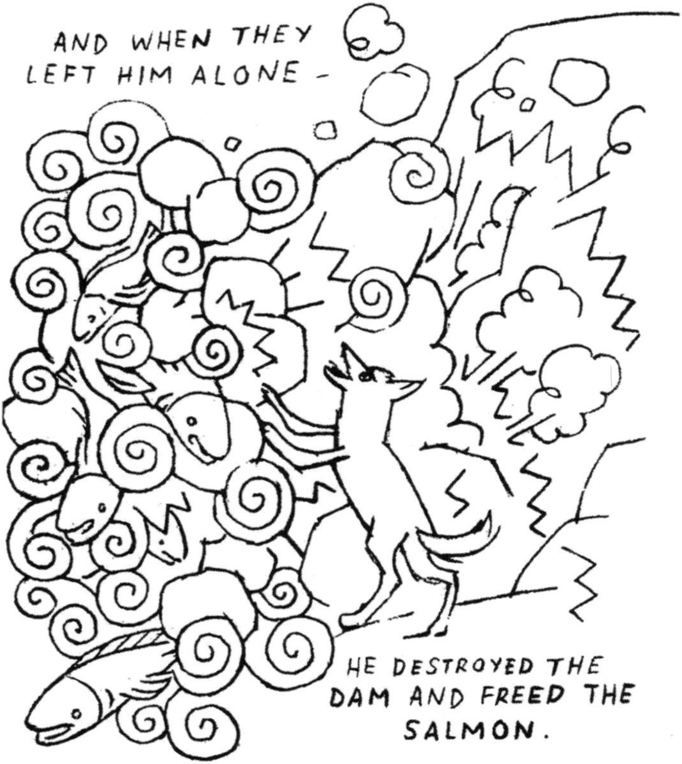
AND WHEN THEY LEFT HIM ALONE -
HE DESTROYED THE DAM AND FREED THE SALMON.

ROCKS FROM THE DAM CREATED
CELILO FALLS — WYAM —

FOR OVER 10,000 YEARS, THE CENTER
OF HUMAN LIFE ALONG THE COLUMBIA

ON THE ROCKS OF COYOTE'S DAM
THE PEOPLE WAITED WITH NETS
FOR THE SALMON —

TRADING MILLIONS
OF POUNDS OF FISH FOR
GOODS FROM AS FAR AWAY
AS THE GREAT LAKES AND THE
SOUTHWEST PUEBLOS. TRAILS
RADIATED OUT FROM WYAM —

AND THOUSANDS OF INDIANS
GATHERED EVERY YEAR TO FISH -

LEVI HOLT:
"IT GAVE ME A FEELING AND
ASSURED ME THAT ALL INDIAN
PEOPLE HONORED THE SALMON
IN THE SAME WAY."

ON MARCH 25, 1957 THE FALLS
DISAPPEARED ABOVE A NEW DAM.

THE RIVER, THE PEOPLE, AND
THE SALMON WERE CHANGED

IN THE EARLY 1900s CELILO VILLAGE
HAD BEEN A CLUSTER OF HOUSES, DRYING
SHEDS, AND A LONGHOUSE JUST NORTH
OF FISHING SITES AROUND THE FALLS.

GEORGE AGUILAR:

"WE LIVED IN AN OLD,
THREE-ROOM HOUSE..."

"...THE FIRST THING I'D NOTICE..."

"...WAS THE DISTINCTIVE FRAGRANCE OF DRIED SALMON HEADS AND EELS HANGING IN GUNNY SACKS OFF THE LEAN-TO KITCHEN WALL."

IN THE MORNINGS MEN WOULD HEAD OUT TO THEIR FAMILY FISHING SPOT.

FOR CENTURIES THEY HAD STEPPED ALONG THE SLICK ROCKS TO REACH THE PLACES WHERE THEIR FATHERS AND GRANDFATHERS HAD DIPPED THEIR NETS INTO THE WATER.

ALFONSE HALFMOON:

"I COULD FEEL MY POLE VIBRATE — THEN, BAM — — A HIT!"

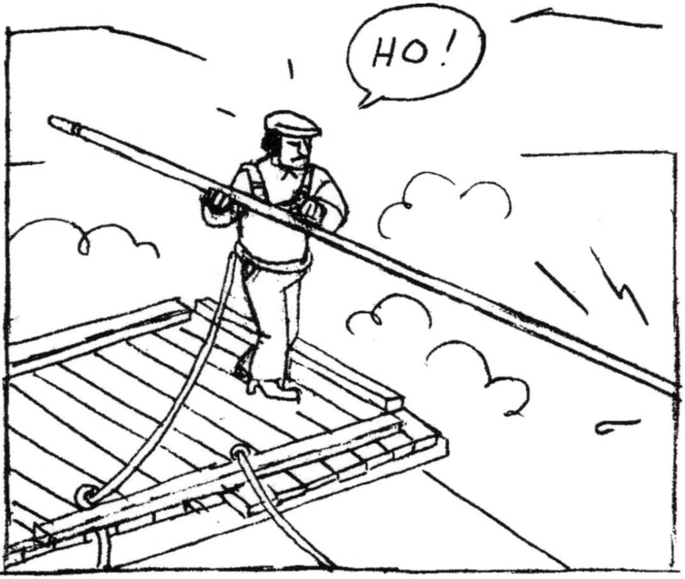
HO!

"EVEN BEFORE I PULLED THE SALMON IN —

— I COULD SMELL THE ODOR OF CHINOOK."

THE SEUFERT BROS. CANNERY BUILT CABLE CARS OVER THE SWIFT WATER IN THE 1930s

INDIANS AT WYAM CONSUMED AND SOLD 2.5 MILLION POUNDS OF SALMON ANNUALLY.

THE WOMEN WERE IN CHARGE OF
CUTTING UP AND PRESERVING FISH.
ELSIE DAVID:

"I'VE HAD a
LOT of TEACHERS;
MY MOM TAUGHT ME
HOW TO FILLET A FISH.
WHEN I GOT OLDER,
MY SISTER TAUGHT ME
HOW TO DRY IT."

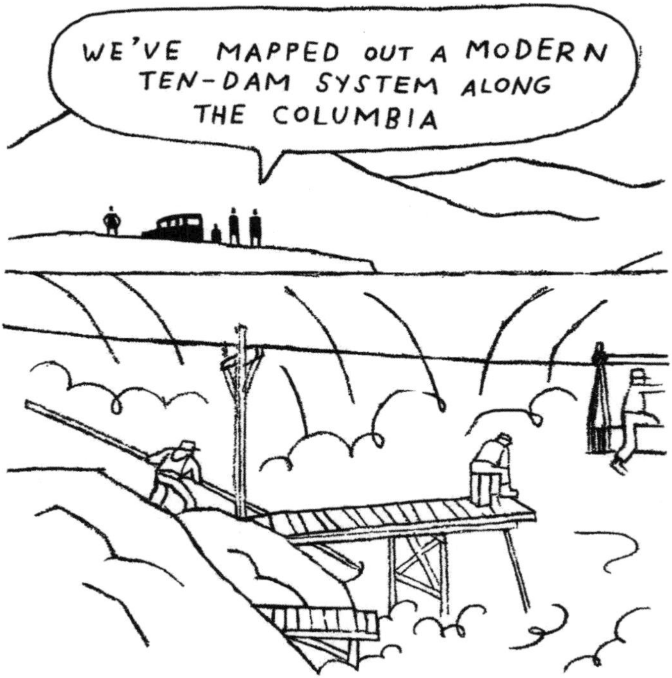
WE'VE MAPPED OUT A MODERN TEN-DAM SYSTEM ALONG THE COLUMBIA

IN THE 1930s THE US ARMY CORPS OF ENGINEERS BEGAN EYEING WYAM

ENGINEER JOHN H. LEWIS:

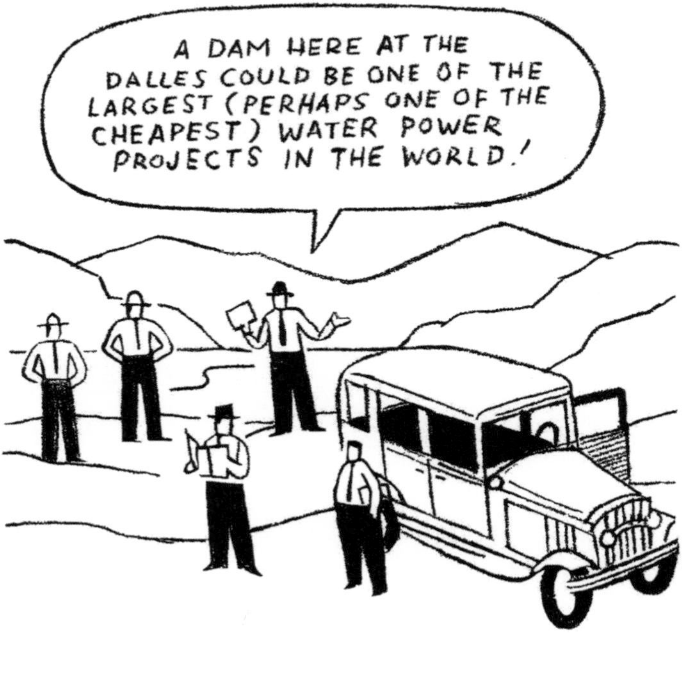
A DAM HERE AT THE DALLES COULD BE ONE OF THE LARGEST (PERHAPS ONE OF THE CHEAPEST) WATER POWER PROJECTS IN THE WORLD!

DAMMING THE ANCIENT FALLS
COULD TRANSFORM THE REGION —
— EASING RIVER TRAFFIC, CREATING
ELECTRICITY AND STABILIZING
IRRIGATION FOR GIANT FARMS.

THE FIRST DAM ON THE COLUMBIA,
ROCK ISLAND DAM, WAS BUILT IN 1933.

TREATIES SIGNED IN 1855 HAD GUARAN-
TEED TRIBES THE ETERNAL RIGHT TO FISH
ON THE COLUMBIA AT SITES THE DALLES DAM
WOULD WIPE OFF THE MAP.
AS PLANS PROGRESSED —

THE YAKIMA,
NEZ PERCE,
UMATILLA, AND
WARM SPRINGS TRIBES
CAMPAIGNED WITH
VARIOUS WHITE
ALLIES AGAINST IT.
BUT COMMERCIAL
INTERESTS PREVAILED...

... AND A MASSIVE 1948 FLOOD, WHICH DESTROYED PORTLAND'S NEIGHBORING CITY, VANPORT, SEALED THE DEAL.

IN 1950, CONGRESS AUTHORIZED THE DALLES DAM. $27 MILLION WAS PAID TO THE TRIBES AS COMPENSATION FOR THE LOSS OF THEIR FISHING SITES AND ANCESTRAL HOMES.

"LIFE IS CHANGING RAPIDLY AND THE LOSS OF ANCIENT FISHING GROUNDS IS BUT ANOTHER STEP IN THE TRANSITION TO A NEW, BEWILDERING EXISTENCE."

— STATE RESEARCHER ANTHONY NETBOY

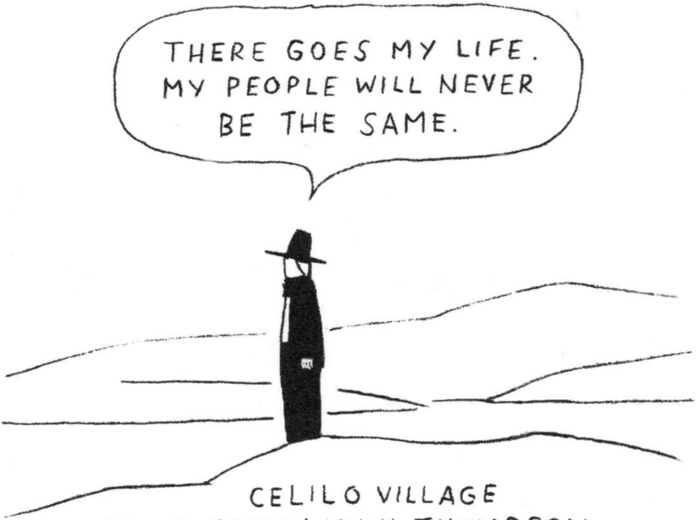
THERE GOES MY LIFE. MY PEOPLE WILL NEVER BE THE SAME.

CELILO VILLAGE CHIEF TOMMY KUNI THOMPSON RESISTED THE NEGOTIATIONS WITH THE ARMY CORPS AND REFUSED THE GOVERNMENT'S MONEY. THE DAM CONSTRUCTION PROCEEDED.

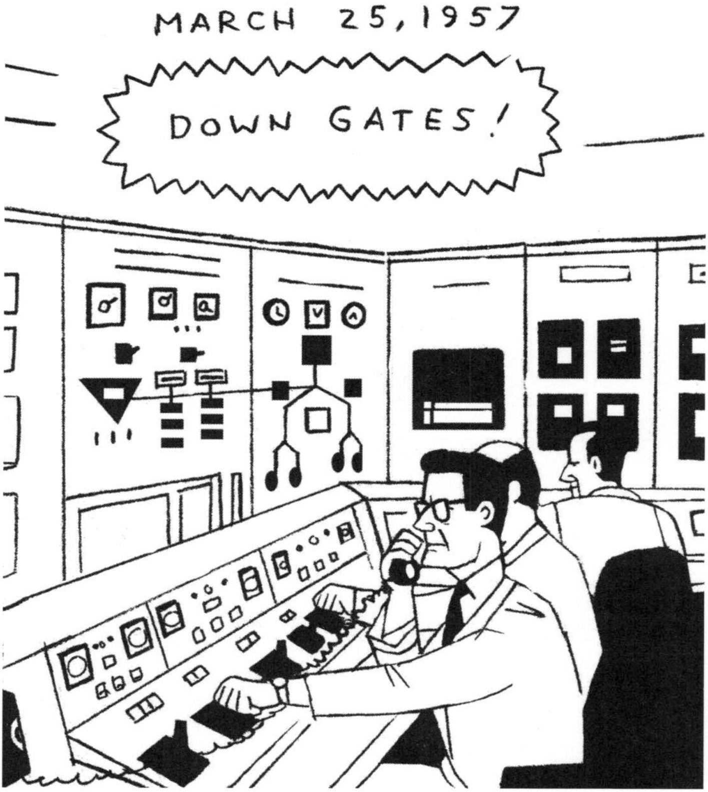
MARCH 25, 1957
DOWN GATES!

IT TOOK TEN MINUTES

FOR THE DAM TO SHUT OFF

THE FLOW of THE COLUMBIA

THE ARMY CORPS BUILT A NEW CELILO
VILLAGE OUTSIDE OF THE FLOOD ZONE
BUT NEGLECTED TO UPGRADE WATER
AND ELECTRICITY STANDARDS UNTIL
2005; A NEW LONGHOUSE—PROMISED
TO THE COMMUNITY 50 YEARS EARLIER

WAS FINALLY ERECTED IN 2009. AND
WHILE CELILO VILLAGE IS OCCUPIED
YEAR-ROUND, LIFE HAS CHANGED—

—ESPECIALLY FOR THE SALMON, WHOSE ROUTES TO SPAWNING STREAMS HAVE BEEN PERMANENTLY ALTERED BY DAMS THROUGHOUT THE COLUMBIA.

THE SALMON MAY NEVER RECOVER.

TODAY, PEOPLE SEEK SOLACE IN THE STILLNESS OF THE REGION'S VANISHING WILDERNESS. BUT CELILO FALLS IS NOW A QUIET FACADE, A MEMORY DROWNED BY MEN WHO CONSIDER NATURE A FORCE TO BE TAMED AND TRAFFICKED.

ALLEN PINKHAM:

"I HAVE STOPPED AT CELILO
OVER THE YEARS AND THE
SILENCE IS A TERRIBLE
THING TO EXPERIENCE;

THERE ARE NO SOUNDS OF
MOTHERS OR GRANDMOTHERS
COOKING.

NO SOUNDS OF MEN
CHOPPING WOOD,

NO SOUNDS OF CHILDREN
RUNNING, PLAYING AND
SHOUTING TO EACH OTHER."

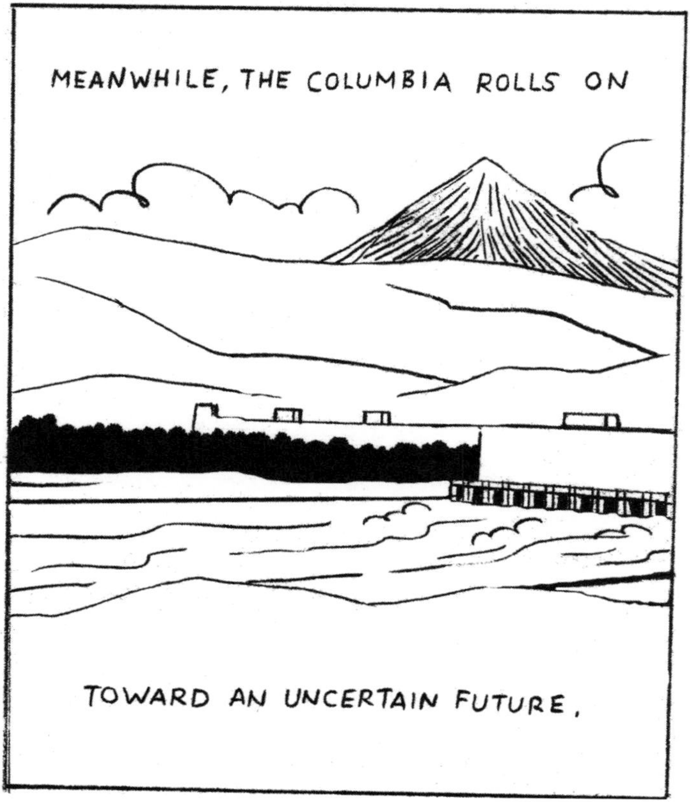
MEANWHILE, THE COLUMBIA ROLLS ON
TOWARD AN UNCERTAIN FUTURE.

Not a Place to Visit.

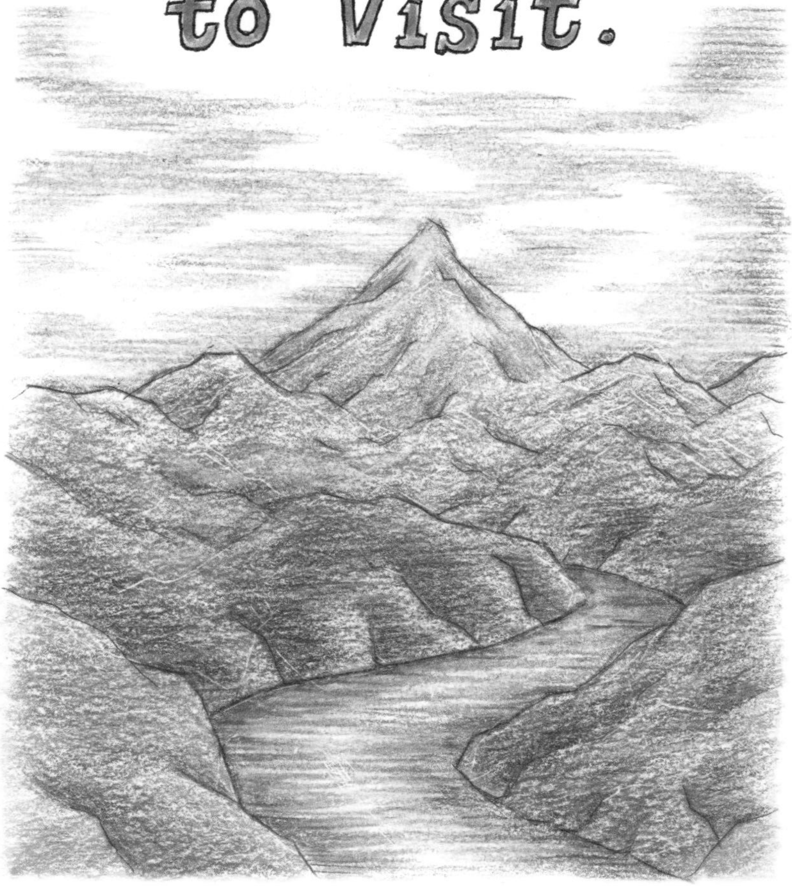

Nature is not a place
to visit. It is home.

Gary Snyder

SOMETIMES I WORK AS A PORTER ABOARD a REPLICA Sternwheeler ON The COLUMBIA RIVER

The position involves the performance of VARIOUS **DUTIES** – HAULING AND STOCKING SUPPLIES AROUND THE SHIP, CLEANING AND Light MAINTENANCE, ROOM SERVICE, and OCCASIONAL **GALLEY** OR **HOUSE-KEEPING** ASSISTANCE.

IT CAN BE TOUGH WORK – 12 HOUR SHIFTS CLAMBERING UP AND DOWN THROUGH 4 DECKS ALL DAY.

The relative ISOLATION of the RIVER and the illusion of SOLITUDE is anodyne.

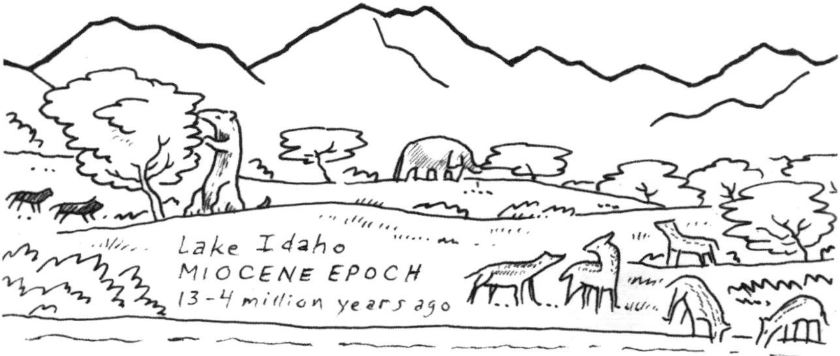
Lake Idaho
MIOCENE EPOCH
13-4 million years ago

The people I work alongside are thoughtful, intelligent, and HARDWORKING. BUT THE VESSEL ITSELF is a MICROCOSM of GLOBAL capitalism, LITTLE MORE THAN a SYMBOL of CONTRIVED NOSTALGIA DESIGNED

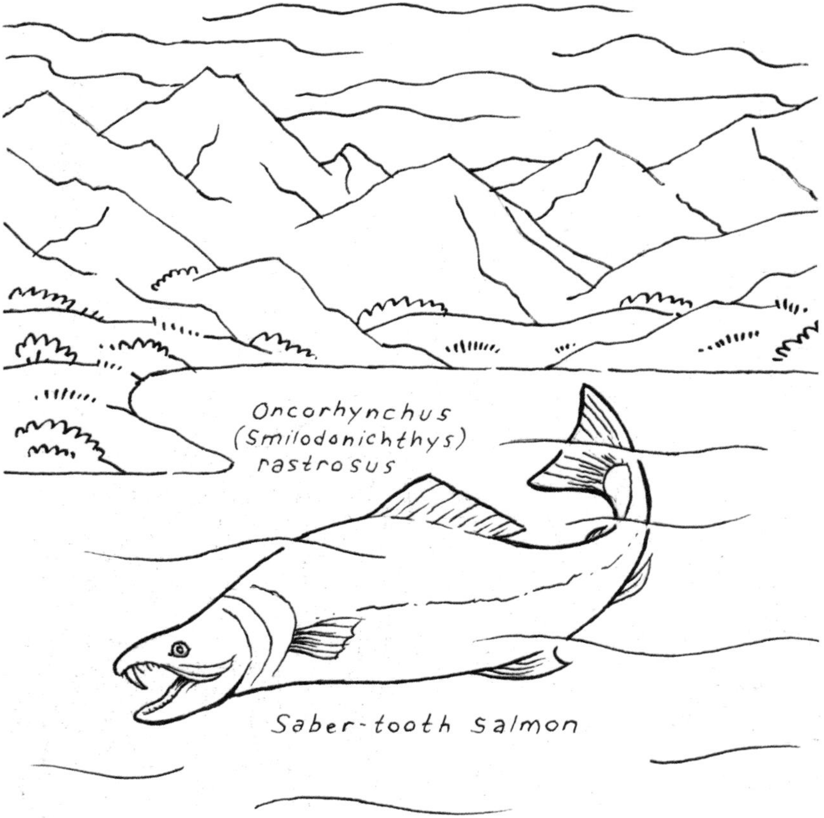

Oncorhynchus (Smilodonichthys) rastrosus
Saber-tooth salmon

TO ECLIPSE the **Nature** of THE **RIVER** ~ THE ship is driven (by "HIDDEN" ENGINES operating beneath the SURFACE) THRU A DEVASTATED **ENVIRONMENT** TOWARDS NO REAL DESTINATION.

The paddlewheel conjures an affectation of GRAND TRADITION ~ BUT

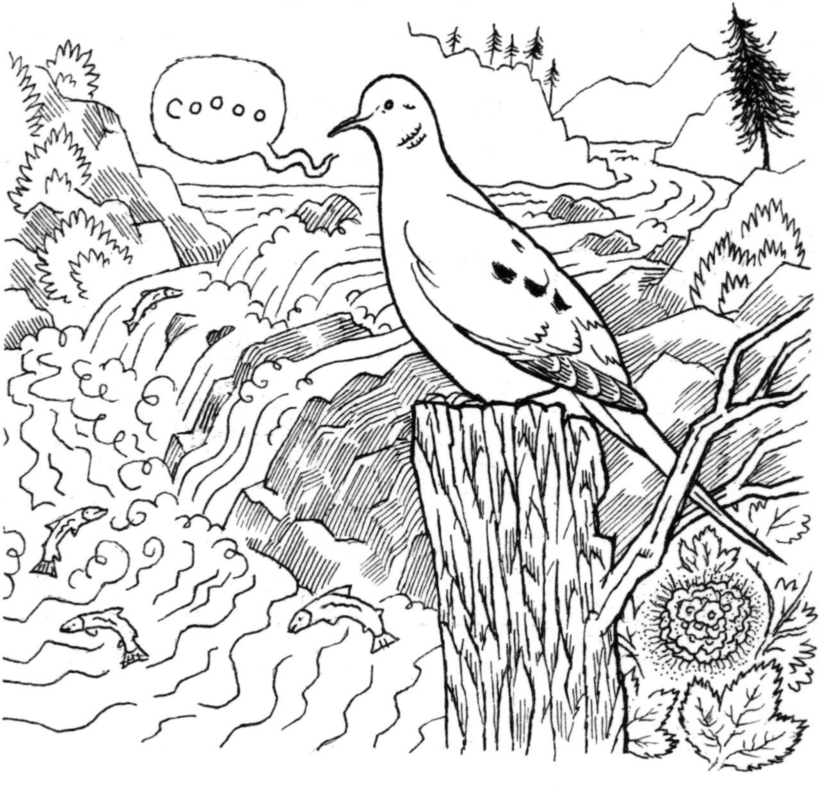
COoooo

PROVIDES VERY LITTLE IN the WAY of **ACTUAL** PROPULSION ～～～

The passenger **SERVICE CREW** is A DIVERSE CONFLUENCE of BACKGROUNDS AND GENDERS, WHILE MOST of the OFFICERS ARE STRAIGHT, WHITE MALES, AND the **MAJORITY** of THE PASSENGERS ARE WEALTHY, WHITE, ELDERLY U.S. **TOURISTS.**

The ship's route follows a course ORIGINALLY MAPPED by LEWIS & CLARK, FROM the **SNAKE** RIVER IN IDAHO — DOWN through THE LOWER COLUMBIA TO

ASTORIA ~ WHERE THE RIVER CHURNS ~ into THE Pacific.

"This river we suppose to be the S. fork of the COLUMBIA, and the fish **THE SALMON** —

— with which we are informed the Columbia River **abounds.**"
— **MERIWETHER LEWIS** August 13 1805

PADDLEWHEEL SHIPS HAVE BEEN TRANSPORTING CARGO AND PASSENGERS UP AND DOWN The COLUMBIA RIVER SINCE THE MID-19TH CENTURY ~

In 1850, the river's first riverine steamship - THE Sidewheeler "COLUMBIA" - launched from Astoria, where LEWIS & CLARK arrived at the conclusion of their expedition 45 years earlier.

As the river is the heart of the region so the

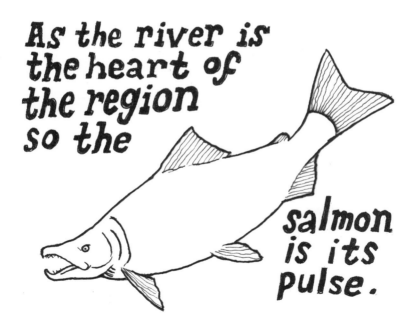

salmon is its pulse.

AFTER THEIR MATURE BODIES ACCUMULATE NUTRIENTS and MARINE-DERIVED NITROGEN from THE OCEAN, these **ANADROMOUS** FISH RETURN TO THEIR ≈ *NATAL STREAMS* TO **SPAWN** AND **DIE**.

THEIR CARCASSES CONTRIBUTE TO THE

Atmospheric NITROGEN

NITROGEN-FIXING MICROBES IN MARINE ENVIRONMENT

Nitrogen budgets of

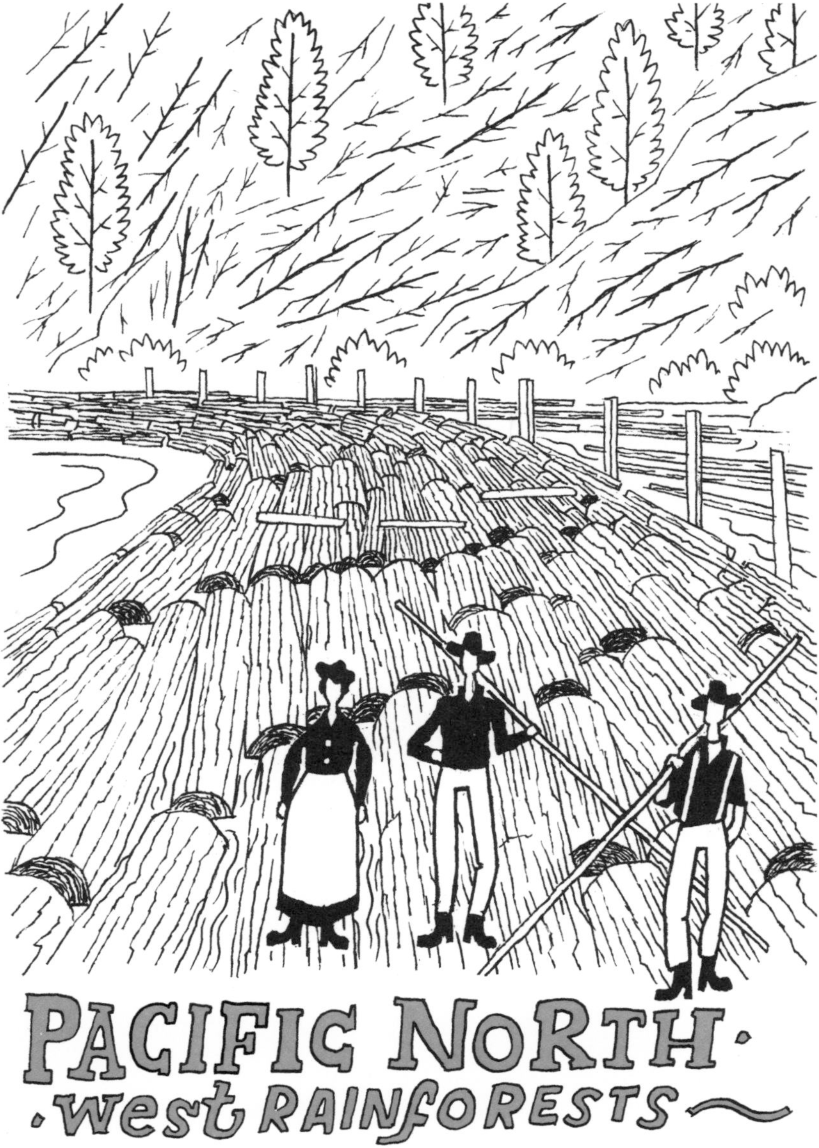

PACIFIC NORTH-west RAINFORESTS

FOR COUNTLESS GENERATIONS THE Columbia's NATIVE COMMUNITIES HAVE BEEN ANCHORED TO THE RIVER'S COMESTIBLE **BOUNTY;**

Sacred RIVER·SALMON·HUMAN RELATIONSHIPS ARE DEMONSTRATED BY CEREMONIES ·THAT· HONOR SALMON

- AND "CODE ECOLOGICAL KNOWLEDGE WHICH CONNECTS -

indigenous people
to the place from
which they come."

–Raymond Pierotti

IN the 20th century

THESE TRADITIONS, bound to the

ANCIENT CONTINUUM

of SALMON MIGRATION at sites LIKE CELILO FALLS,

WERE DISRUPTED BY THE CONSTRUCTION of the COLUMBIA'S MODERN DAM SYSTEM.

THE IMPOSITION of "PLACELESS HARVEST" MANAGEMENT PRACTICES

BASED UPON INDUSTRIAL MODELS RATHER THAN SPECIES RANGE DYNAMICS FURTHER FRAGMENTED THE Salmon's LIFE-HISTORY HABITAT CHAIN

"While we were busy transforming **SALMON INTO PRODUCT,**" WRITES SALMON BIOLOGIST *Jim Lichatowich,* "WE FAILED TO NOTICE THAT WE WERE AT THE Same Time DIMINISHING THEIR ANNUAL RETURN To the **RIVERS OF THE PACIFIC NORTHWEST** — KILLING OUR **PLACE-DEFINING EVENT...**

PRODUCT IS ANOTHER STEP in the EROSION of OUR SENSE of PLACE."

The erasure of salmon places — and

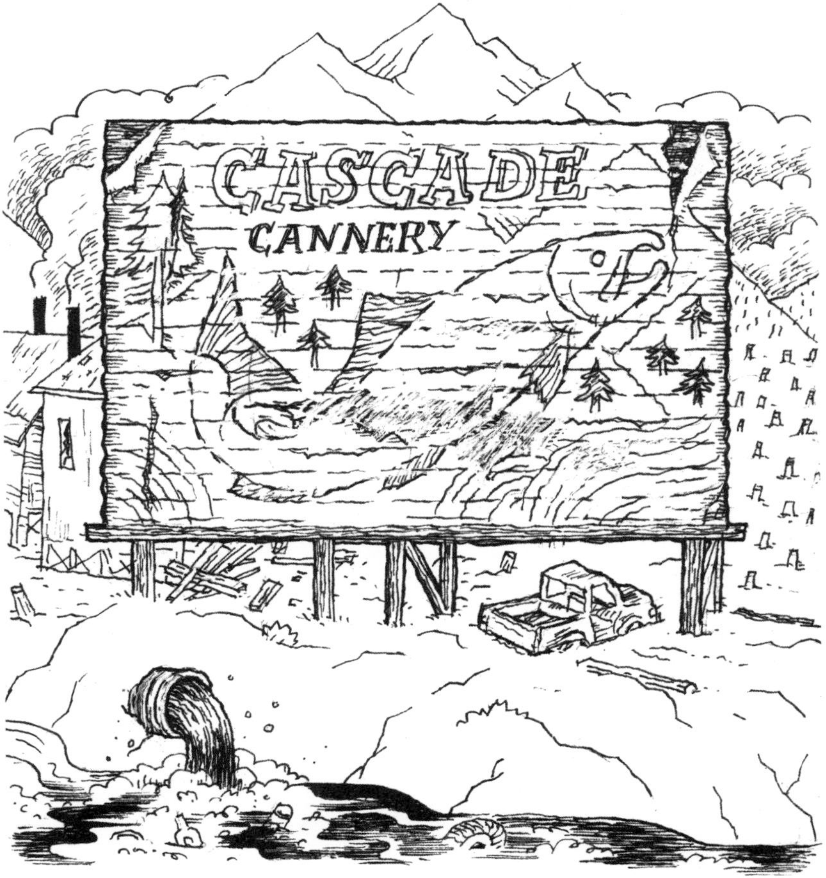

CASCADE
CANNERY

THEIR CONVERSION
BY CAPITALIST CONCEIT
FROM LIVING HABITAT
TO CONCEPTUAL PROPERTY ~
RESULTED IN THE DISPLACEMENT OF
SALMON PEOPLE AND THE

DECIMATION OF SALMON
THROUGHOUT THE REGION.

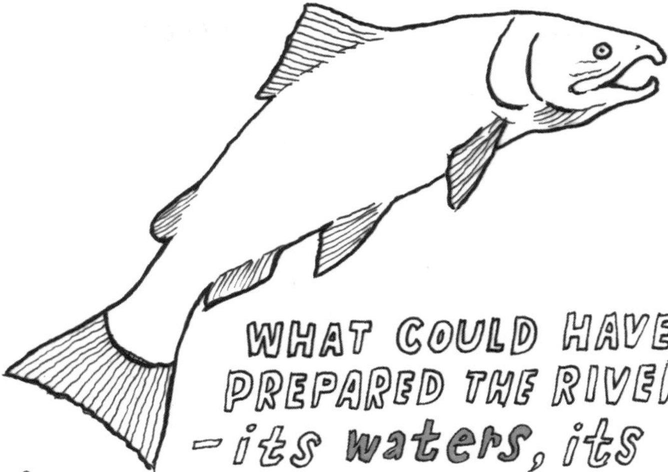

WHAT COULD HAVE PREPARED THE RIVER – its **waters**, its fishes, forests, and **people** – FOR THE DEVASTATION delivered by the CAPRICIOUS **COYOTE** IN HIS DISGUISE AS THE TIMBER INDUSTRY, THE COMMERCIAL **fishing** trade, THE DAMS, THE TOURISTS?

I can offer nothing more than a USELESS APOLOGY for my complicity.

THE REGION'S WHITE EUROPEAN-ORIGIN
SETTLERS IMAGINED THEMSELVES INGENIOUS
MASTERS of The NATURAL WORLD —
INDUSTRIAL ERA ENGINE-BUILDERS WHOSE
INVENTIONS and ENLIGHTENMENT PHILOSOPHY
DEMARCATED A BORDER BETWEEN HUMAN
BIOLOGY AND THE ENVIRONMENT.

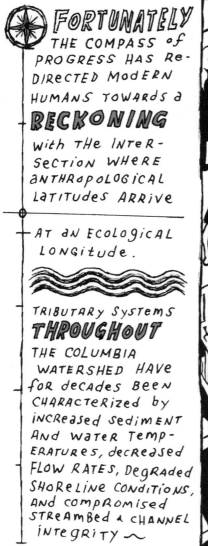

FORTUNATELY THE COMPASS of PROGRESS HAS RE-DIRECTED MODERN HUMANS TOWARDS a **RECKONING** with THE INTERSECTION WHERE ANTHROPOLOGICAL LATITUDES ARRIVE

AT AN ECOLOGICAL LONGITUDE.

TRIBUTARY SYSTEMS **THROUGHOUT** THE COLUMBIA WATERSHED HAVE FOR DECADES BEEN CHARACTERIZED by INCREASED SEDIMENT AND WATER TEMPERATURES, DECREASED FLOW RATES, DEGRADED SHORELINE CONDITIONS, AND COMPROMISED STREAMBED & CHANNEL INTEGRITY ~

What cost does the environment pay for my work ?

FISH AND WILDLIFE OFFICIALS WITH THE CONFEDERATED TRIBES of the COLVILLE RESERVATION are currently awaiting a NOAA* PERMIT ALLOWING THE RE-INTRODUCTION of HATCHERY SPRING CHINOOK TO UPPER COLUMBIA REACHES ABOVE THE GRAND COULEE AND CHIEF JOSEPH DAMS.

MEANWHILE, THE INDUSTRY OF RIVER TOURISM-of A PIECE WITH THE DISASTROUS LEGACY OF EUROPEAN SETTLEMENT IN NORTH AMERICA- MARKETS an experience of STRAINING ONE'S EARS AT THE IMAGINED ECHOES of A VANISHED WORLD

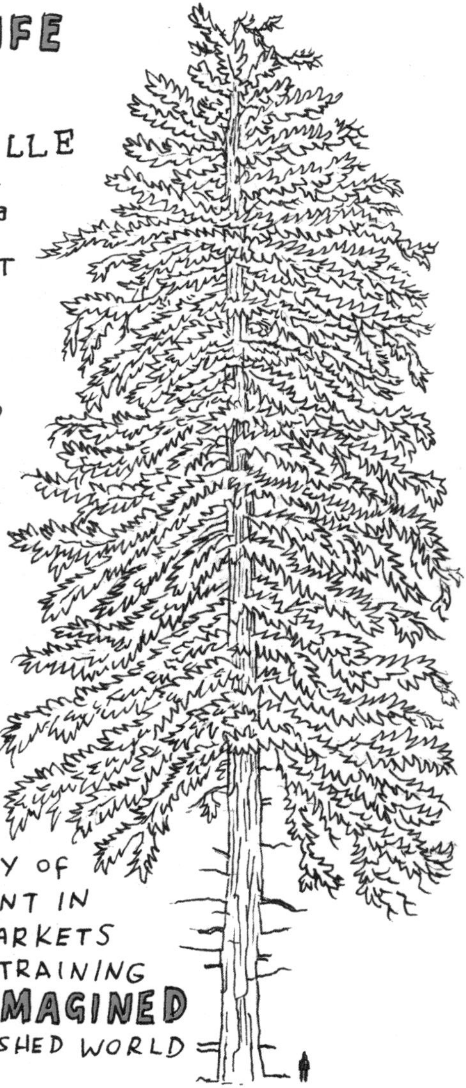

*National Oceanographic and Atmospheric Administration

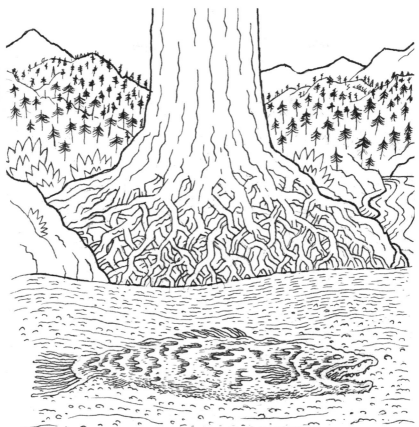

TO FETISHIZE THE **SACRED** PLACES
of **INDIGENOUS** PEOPLES.

AND WHERE WOULD AMERICANS BE
WITHOUT THEIR HABITS of CONSUMPTION?
IS IT EASIER TO IMAGINE THE END of
THE WORLD THAN TO IMAGINE
THE END of **CAPITALISM?**

After DOZING through A PRESENTATION by A TRIBAL **NEZ PERCE** STORYTELLER, PASSENGERS ON THE SHIP MAKE THEIR WAY BACK TO STATEROOMS THEY'VE PAID THOUSANDS of **DOLLARS** TO OCCUPY for THE WEEK-LONG CRUISE.

SOMEONE USUALLY PAUSES TO **LINGER** OVER IMAGES IN ONE of THE **GALLERIES**

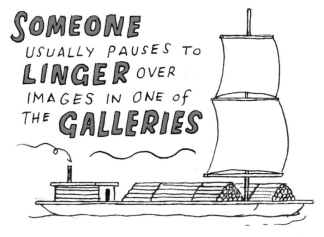

OF PACIFIC NORTHWEST ART HANGING IN THE DECK CORRIDORS.

THE NATIVE AMERICAN TEN COMMANDMENTS IS A PERENNIAL FAVORITE.

"Those indians," someone sheepishly faux-drawls an attempt to squelch the deafening silence of shame ~~~~

"They sure were wise."

And everyone within earshot nods, virtue-signaling their assent. But then they've missed out on an hour of *FOX NEWS* messaging — and they scurry diligently off to the

TELEVISION SETS in their CABINS.

THE BIZARRE TRAGEDY OF SUCH LIVES IS IMPOSSIBLE TO HONOR.

THEY HAVE BEEN ENTIRELY MISSPENT IN A COLLABORATIVE PERFORMANCE PERPETUATING AMONG THEMSELVES AND THEIR BROOD THE NOTION

THAT PLACE AND EXPERIENCE
ARE COMMODITIES FROM WHICH
SOME SENSE OF MEANING
CAN BE EXTRACTED ~~~

~ LIKE FISH FROM A DAMNED RIVER.

ALWAYS ON

WRITTEN AND DRAWN WINTER
& SPRING 2019, COMPLETED
AUGUST 19, 2019; PORTLAND, OREGON.

JULIA AND I HAD PLANNED ON CREATING A COLLABORATIVE PIECE BASED ON OUR EXPLORATION OF THE SALTON SEA AREA. CIRCUMSTANCES DETERMINED THIS VERSION WOULD BE COMPLETED EXCLUSIVELY FOR THIS BOOK. —tee

There was originally included in ALWAYS ON a rambling explanation about my nickname for Julia — which isn't the only thing excised from this work.

A few years ago Julia and I traveled through rural Pennsylvania exploring old abandoned resorts in the Poconos. When she moved back to the west coast we began planning a road trip to southern California to visit the SALTON Sea.

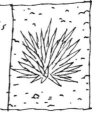

I was interested in developing a comic that explored the friendship between characters moving through a devastated natural environment. Humans in the anthropocene.

Drawing characters in a comic like this is one thing; drawing or representing another cartoonist who also draws auto-biographical comics is an altogether different thing — especially situating the scenario in an ecosystem with a severely threatened biodiversity.

Anyhow Julia is a hilarious and gracious human being and we have been friends for many years. There were times when I felt while working on this that my convoluted creative process would jeopardize our friendship. I am happy to report that we survived this comic.

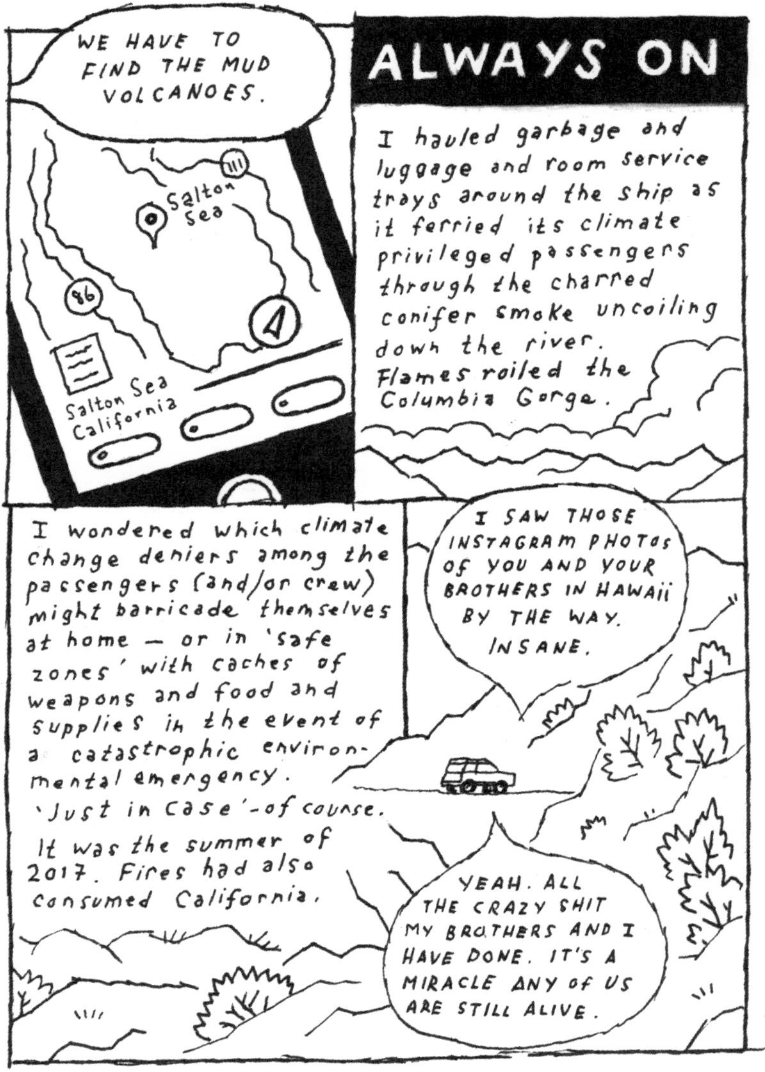
WE HAVE TO FIND THE MUD VOLCANOES.
Salton Sea
111
86
Salton Sea California
ALWAYS ON
I hauled garbage and luggage and room service trays around the ship as it ferried its climate privileged passengers through the charred conifer smoke uncoiling down the river. Flames roiled the Columbia Gorge.
I wondered which climate change deniers among the passengers (and/or crew) might barricade themselves at home — or in 'safe zones' with caches of weapons and food and supplies in the event of a catastrophic environmental emergency.
'Just in case'-of course.
It was the summer of 2017. Fires had also consumed California.
I SAW THOSE INSTAGRAM PHOTOS OF YOU AND YOUR BROTHERS IN HAWAII BY THE WAY. INSANE.
YEAH. ALL THE CRAZY SHIT MY BROTHERS AND I HAVE DONE. IT'S A MIRACLE ANY OF US ARE STILL ALIVE.

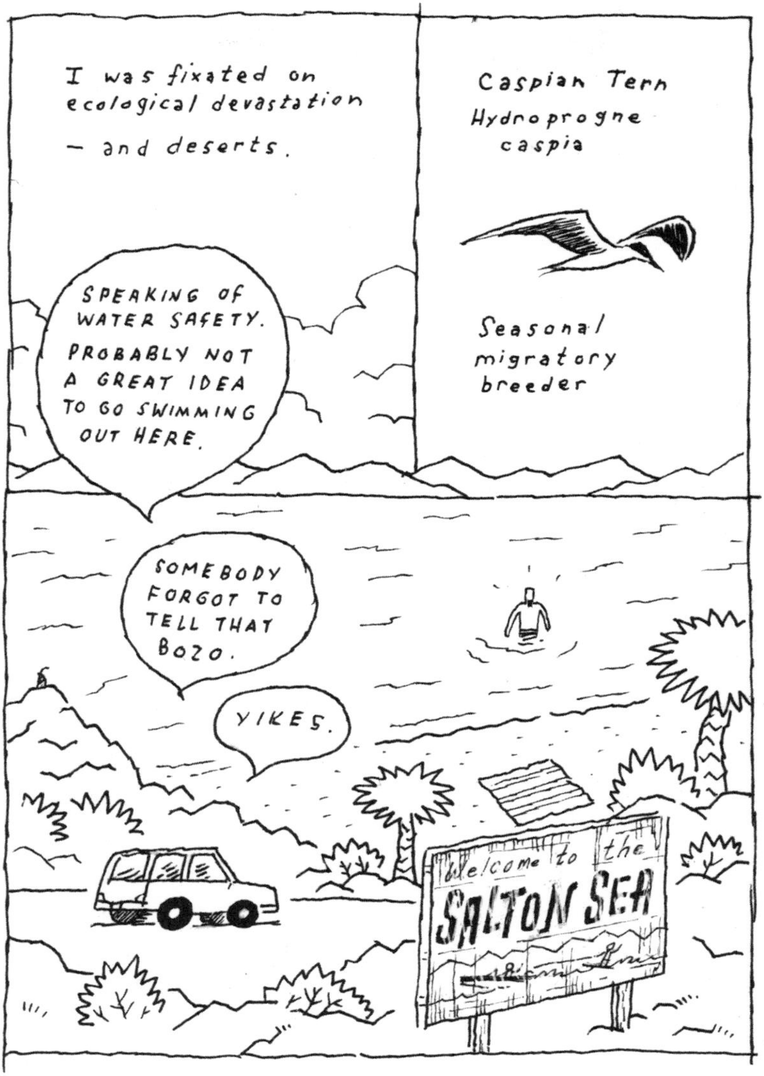
I was fixated on ecological devastation
— and deserts.
SPEAKING OF WATER SAFETY.
PROBABLY NOT A GREAT IDEA TO GO SWIMMING OUT HERE.
Caspian Tern
Hydroprogne caspia
Seasonal migratory breeder
SOMEBODY FORGOT TO TELL THAT BOZO.
YIKES.
Welcome to the
SALTON SEA

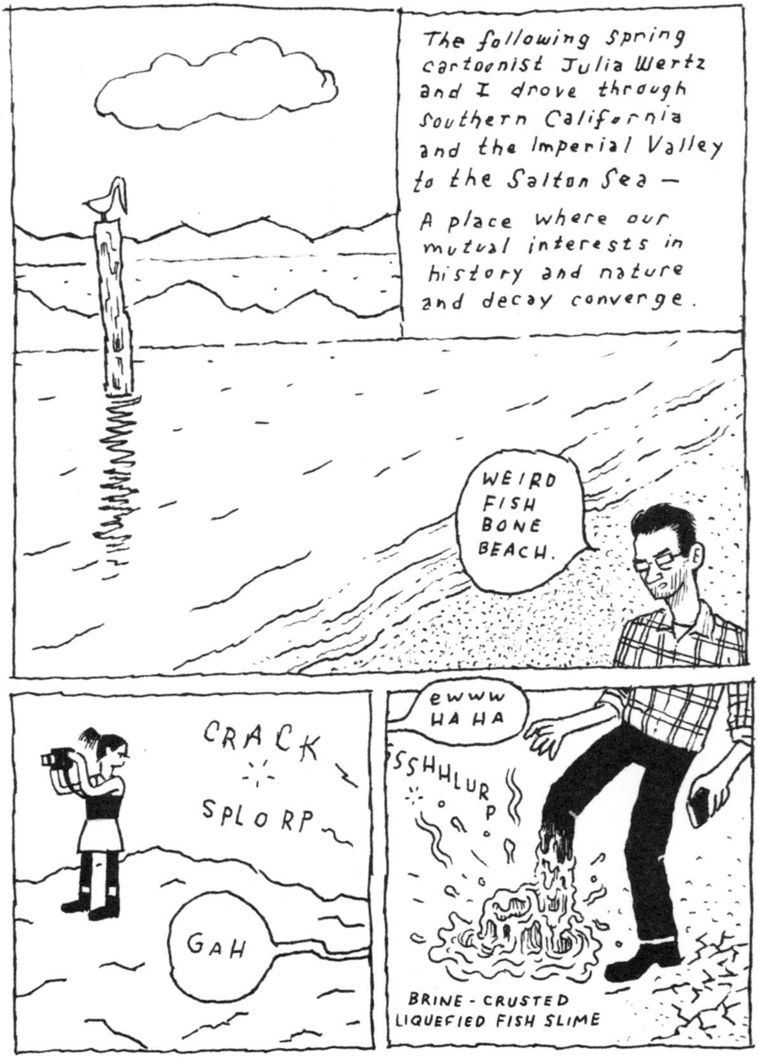
The following spring cartoonist Julia Wertz and I drove through Southern California and the Imperial Valley to the Salton Sea —
A place where our mutual interests in history and nature and decay converge.
WEIRD FISH BONE BEACH.
CRACK
SPLORP
GAH
ewww HA HA
SSHHLURP
BRINE-CRUSTED LIQUEFIED FISH SLIME

Years ago I would travel to Tuscon to visit a woman whose gift to me was her belief in the magic of the desert.
An omen once crossed her yard overhead – in the shape of an owl, she said.
Sometimes in the early evenings we went west past the edge of town over the mountain to bask in the coral dusk and radiant shadows of the Sonoran.
–ARCHAEOLOGISTS TRACE USAGE OF THE MATERIAL FROM THIS EXPOSED SITE BETWEEN 8400–500 YEARS AGO.
THIS OBSIDIAN BUTTE IS RELATIVELY YOUNG.
UNLIKE US.
Western Burrowing Owl
Athene cunicularia
·Local resident
·Recommended for endangered or threatened species status
AW, LOOK AT THAT LITTLE GUY!

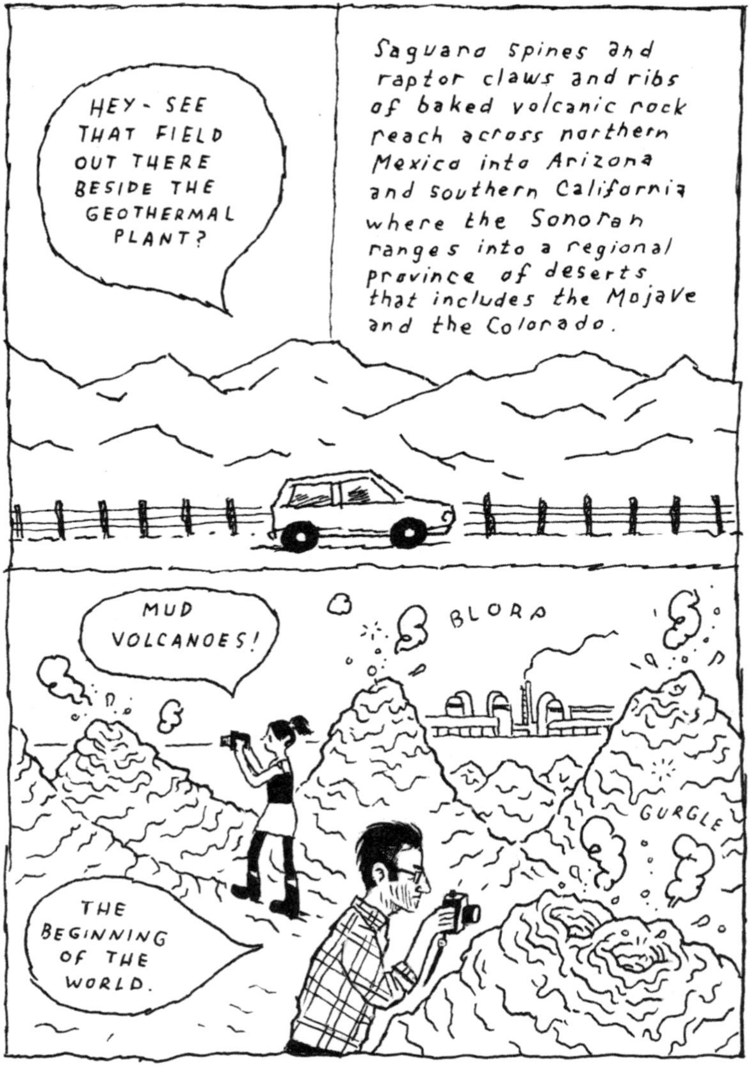

HEY - SEE THAT FIELD OUT THERE BESIDE THE GEOTHERMAL PLANT?
Saguaro spines and raptor claws and ribs of baked volcanic rock reach across northern Mexico into Arizona and southern California where the Sonoran ranges into a regional province of deserts that includes the Mojave and the Colorado.
MUD VOLCANOES!
BLORP
GURGLE
THE BEGINNING OF THE WORLD.

The San Andreas fault and the east Pacific rise directed the Colorado River's passage to the Gulf of Mexico as ages of deposition yielded the fertile terrain that steadily channeled the river through the warm Imperial Valley.
WHOA!
LOOK WHAT THAT TOXIC FISH SLIME DID TO MY LEG—
THE HAIR IS ALL GONE!
WHAT! No way.
LET ME SEE YOUR OTHER LEG.
HA HA!
YOU'RE AN IDIOT.
Naturally bald weird ankles

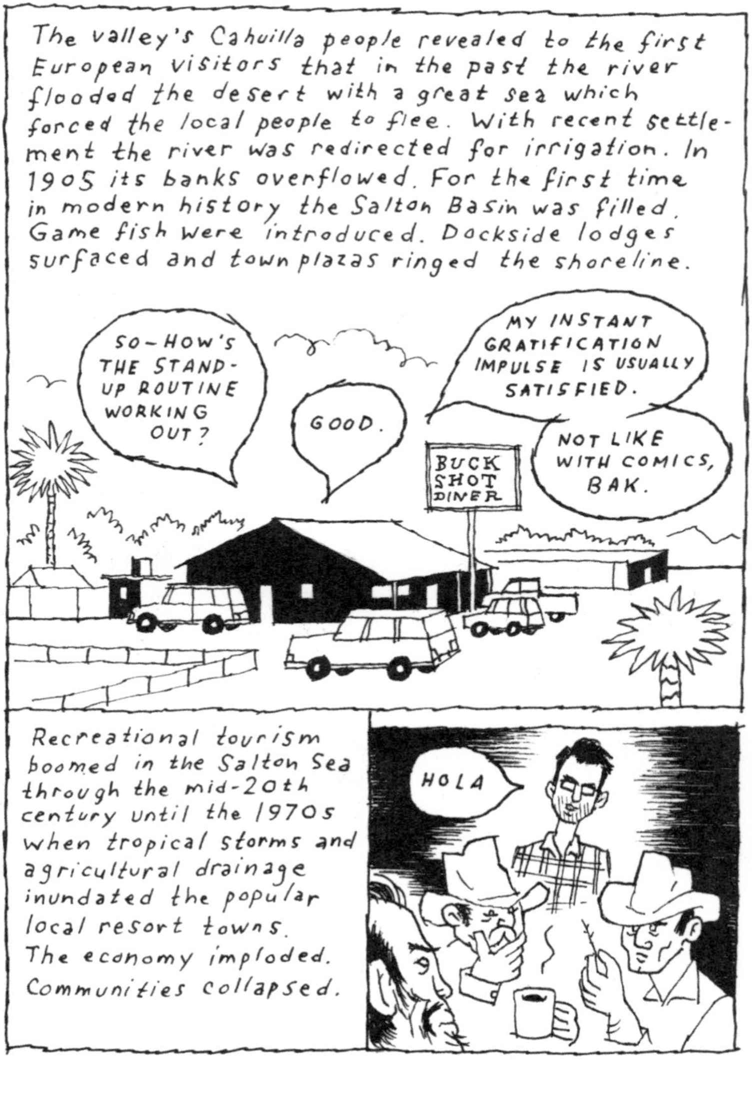
The valley's Cahuilla people revealed to the first European visitors that in the past the river flooded the desert with a great sea which forced the local people to flee. With recent settlement the river was redirected for irrigation. In 1905 its banks overflowed. For the first time in modern history the Salton Basin was filled. Game fish were introduced. Dockside lodges surfaced and town plazas ringed the shoreline.
SO—HOW'S THE STAND-UP ROUTINE WORKING OUT?
GOOD.
MY INSTANT GRATIFICATION IMPULSE IS USUALLY SATISFIED.
NOT LIKE WITH COMICS, BAK.
BUCK SHOT DINER
Recreational tourism boomed in the Salton Sea through the mid-20th century until the 1970s when tropical storms and agricultural drainage inundated the popular local resort towns. The economy imploded. Communities collapsed.
HOLA

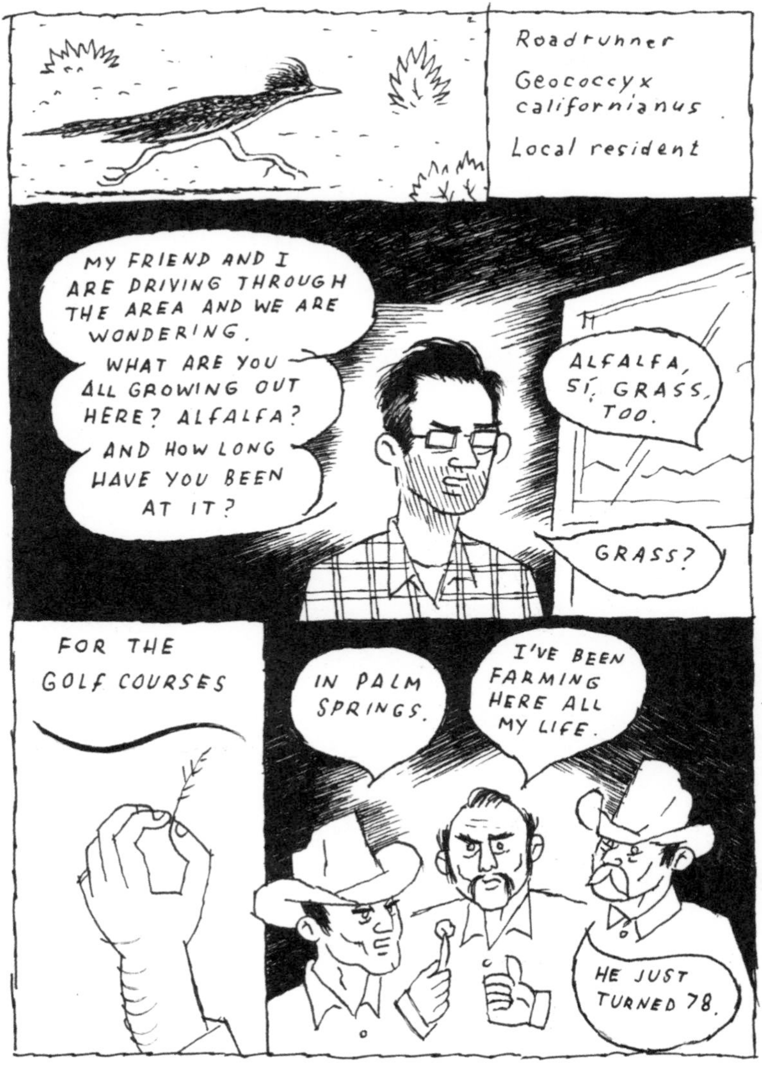
Roadrunner
Geococcyx californianus
Local resident
MY FRIEND AND I ARE DRIVING THROUGH THE AREA AND WE ARE WONDERING.
WHAT ARE YOU ALL GROWING OUT HERE? ALFALFA?
AND HOW LONG HAVE YOU BEEN AT IT?
ALFALFA, SÍ, GRASS, TOO.
GRASS?
FOR THE GOLF COURSES
IN PALM SPRINGS.
I'VE BEEN FARMING HERE ALL MY LIFE.
HE JUST TURNED 78.

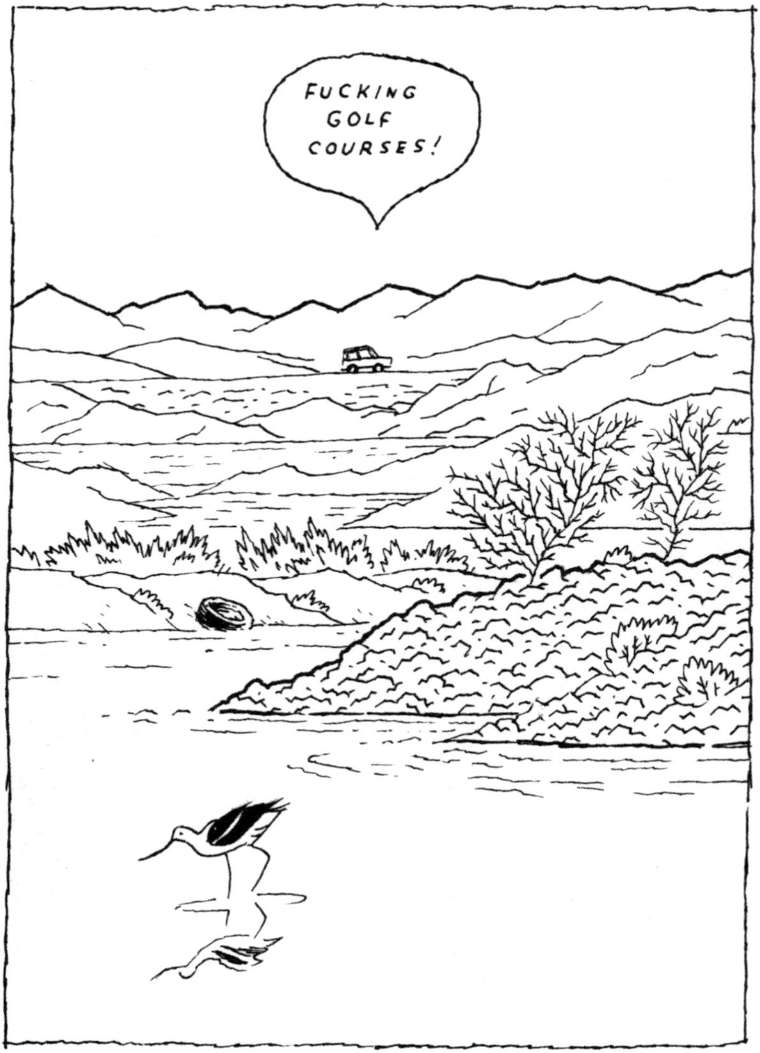
FUCKING GOLF COURSES!

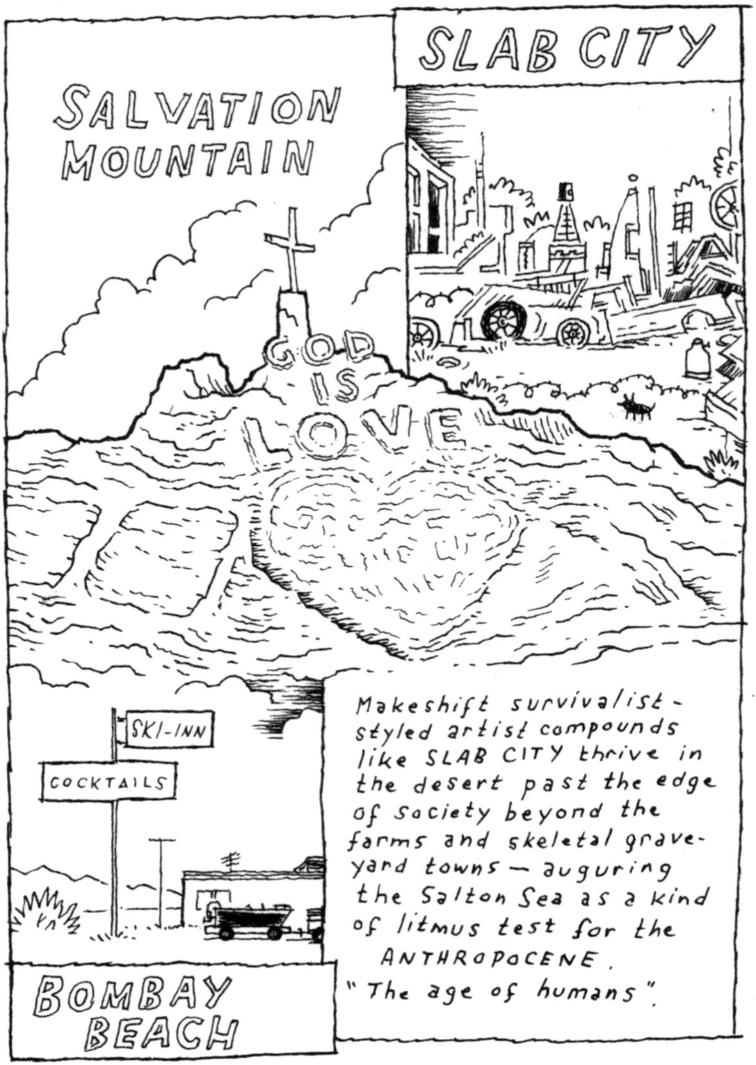
SLAB CITY
SALVATION MOUNTAIN
GOD IS LOVE
SKI-INN
COCKTAILS
Makeshift survivalist-styled artist compounds like SLAB CITY thrive in the desert past the edge of society beyond the farms and skeletal grave-yard towns — auguring the Salton Sea as a kind of litmus test for the ANTHROPOCENE. "The age of humans".
BOMBAY BEACH

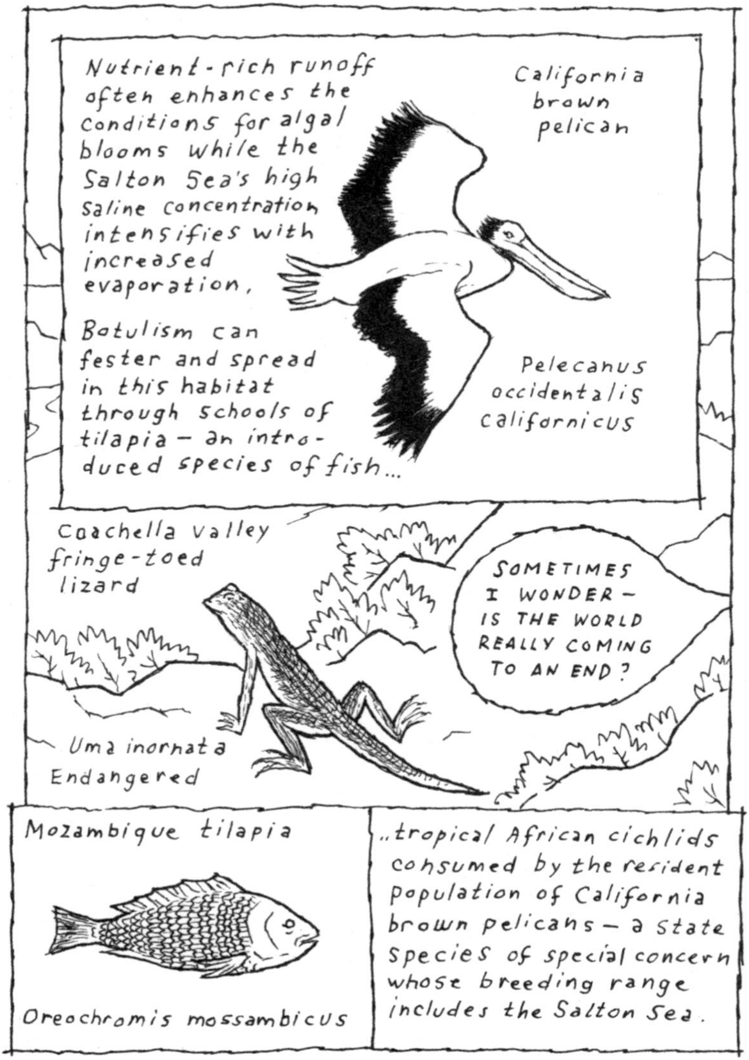

Nutrient-rich runoff often enhances the conditions for algal blooms while the Salton Sea's high saline concentration intensifies with increased evaporation,
California brown pelican
Batulism can fester and spread in this habitat through schools of tilapia – an intro-duced species of fish...
Pelecanus occidentalis californicus
Coachella valley fringe-toed lizard
SOMETIMES I WONDER – IS THE WORLD REALLY COMING TO AN END?
Uma inornata
Endangered
Mozambique tilapia
Oreochromis mossambicus
..tropical African cichlids consumed by the resident population of California brown pelicans – a state species of special concern whose breeding range includes the Salton Sea.

ANYHOW, IT'S ALL JUST EVOLUTION. THERE'S NO NATURAL ORDER.
NO 'NATURAL BALANCE'. NO BEGINNING AND NO END. JUST A PROCESS.
GOTCHA.
ON THE OTHER HAND-
CLIK
-THIS IS A PATH OF OUR OWN DESIGN.
THE WORLD IS NOT
WHAT IT SEEMS.

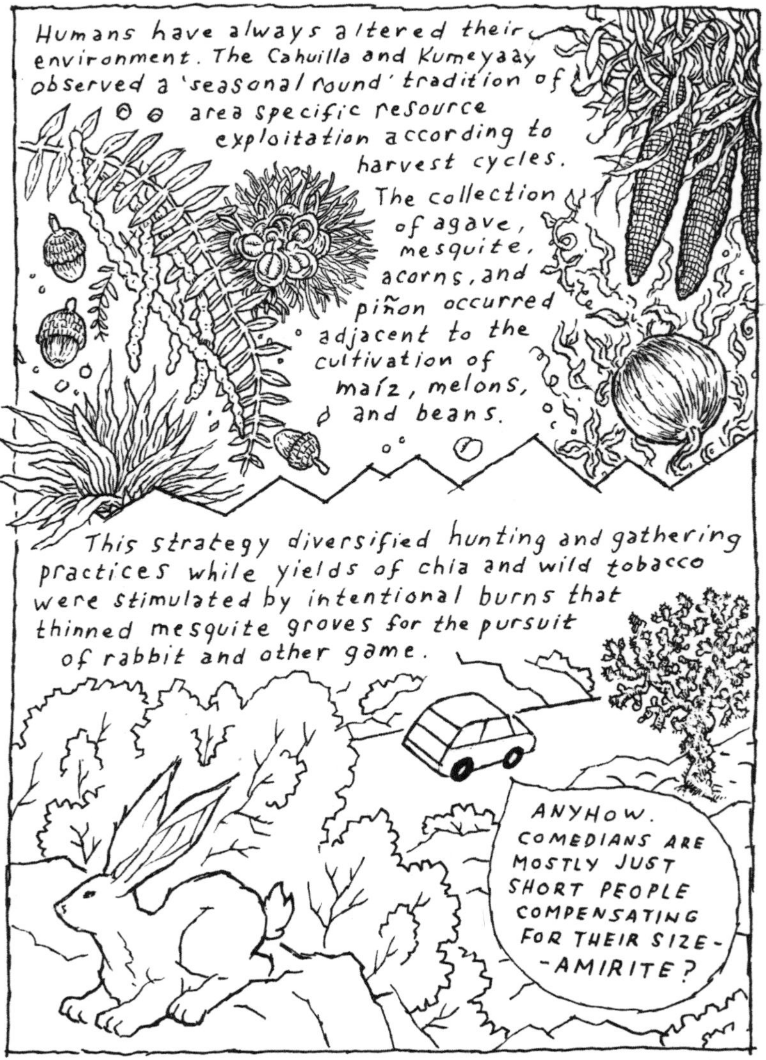
Humans have always altered their environment. The Cahuilla and Kumeyaay observed a 'seasonal round' tradition of area specific resource exploitation according to harvest cycles.
The collection of agave, mesquite, acorns, and piñon occurred adjacent to the cultivation of maíz, melons, and beans.
This strategy diversified hunting and gathering practices while yields of chia and wild tobacco were stimulated by intentional burns that thinned mesquite groves for the pursuit of rabbit and other game.
ANYHOW. COMEDIANS ARE MOSTLY JUST SHORT PEOPLE COMPENSATING FOR THEIR SIZE- -AMIRITE?

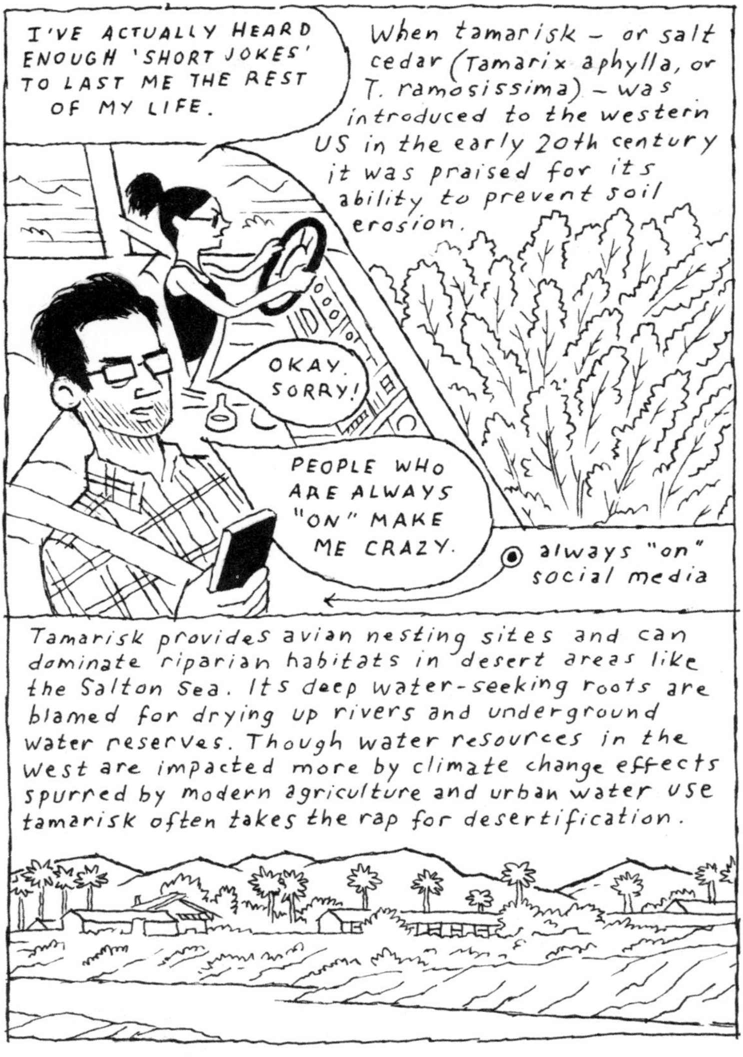
I'VE ACTUALLY HEARD ENOUGH 'SHORT JOKES' TO LAST ME THE REST OF MY LIFE.
When tamarisk – or salt cedar (Tamarix aphylla, or T. ramosissima) – was introduced to the western US in the early 20th century it was praised for its ability to prevent soil erosion.
OKAY. SORRY!
PEOPLE WHO ARE ALWAYS "ON" MAKE ME CRAZY.
always "on" social media
Tamarisk provides avian nesting sites and can dominate riparian habitats in desert areas like the Salton Sea. Its deep water-seeking roots are blamed for drying up rivers and underground water reserves. Though water resources in the west are impacted more by climate change effects spurred by modern agriculture and urban water use tamarisk often takes the rap for desertification.

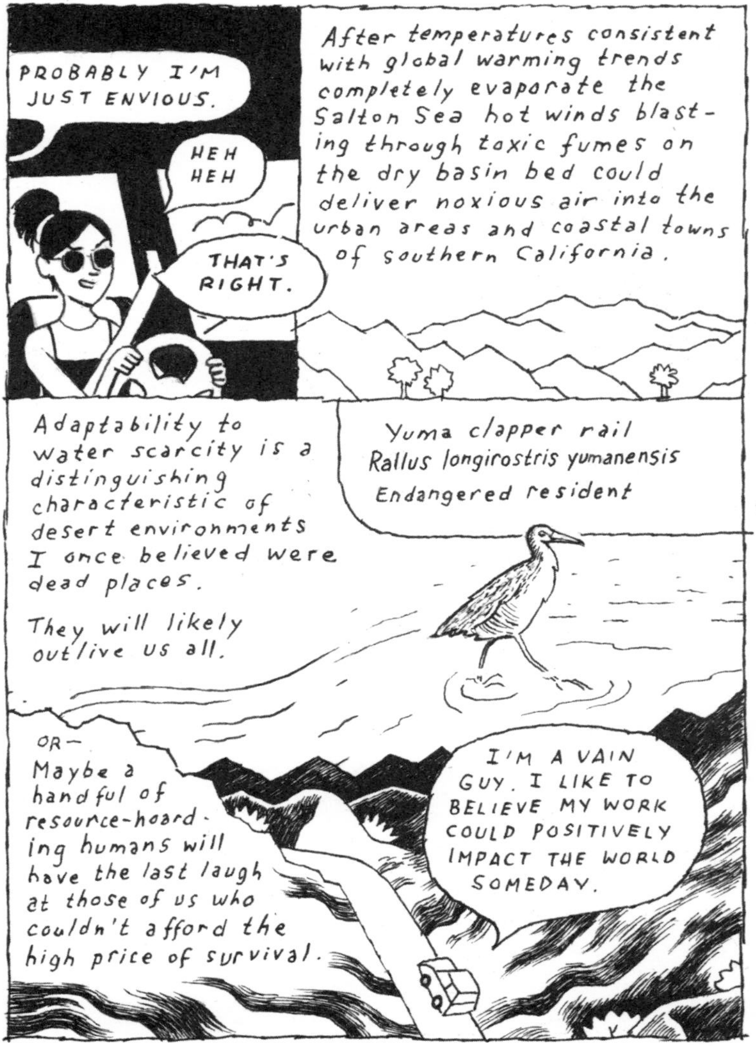
PROBABLY I'M JUST ENVIOUS.
HEH HEH
THAT'S RIGHT.
After temperatures consistent with global warming trends completely evaporate the Salton Sea hot winds blasting through toxic fumes on the dry basin bed could deliver noxious air into the urban areas and coastal towns of southern California.
Adaptability to water scarcity is a distinguishing characteristic of desert environments I once believed were dead places.
They will likely outlive us all.
Yuma clapper rail
Rallus longirostris yumanensis
Endangered resident
OR—
Maybe a handful of resource-hoarding humans will have the last laugh at those of us who couldn't afford the high price of survival.
I'M A VAIN GUY. I LIKE TO BELIEVE MY WORK COULD POSITIVELY IMPACT THE WORLD SOMEDAY.

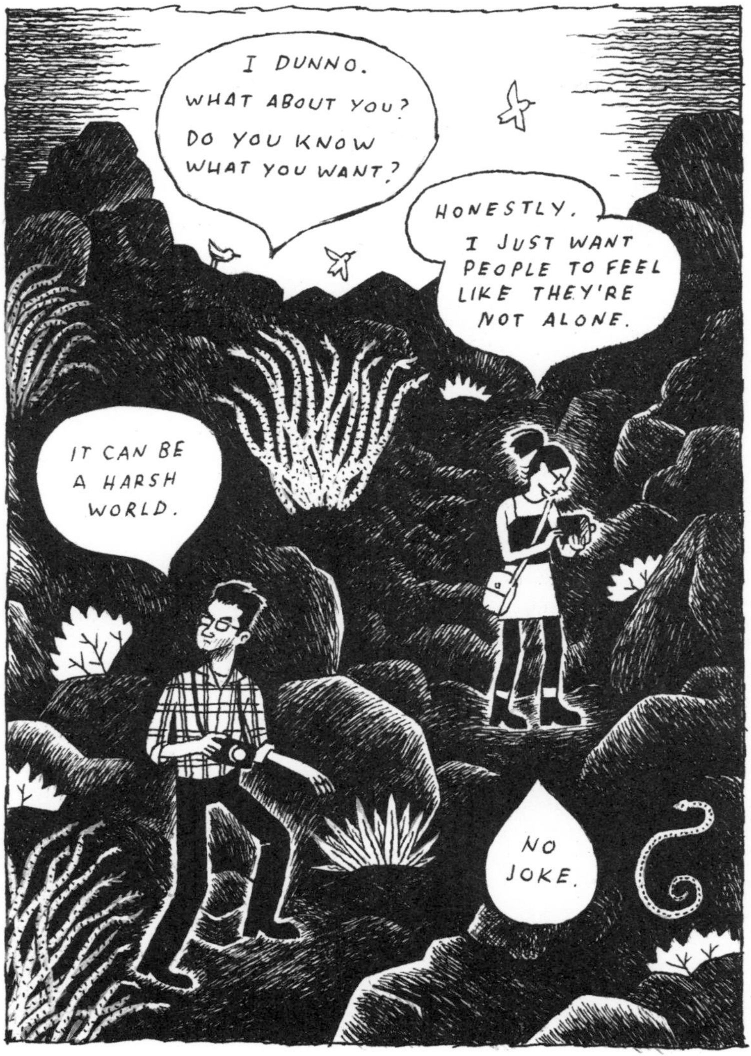
I DUNNO. WHAT ABOUT YOU? DO YOU KNOW WHAT YOU WANT?
HONESTLY. I JUST WANT PEOPLE TO FEEL LIKE THEY'RE NOT ALONE.
IT CAN BE A HARSH WORLD.
NO JOKE.

REFERENCES

Alles, David L. "Geology of the Salton Trough." Western Washington University, 28 October 2011, fire.biol.wwu.edu/trent/alles/Geology SaltonTrough.pdf.

Anzaldua, Gloria. Borderlands/La Frontera: The New Mestiza. Aunt Lute. 1987.

Audubon Society. "Important Bird Areas—Imperial Valley, California." www.audubon.org/important-bird-areas/imperial.valley.

Boyd, Robert T., et al., editors. Chinookan People of the Lower Columbia. University of Washington Press, Seattle and London, 2013.

Engel, Leonard, editor. The Big Empty: Essays on Western Landscapes as Narrative. University of New Mexico Press, Albuquerque, 1994.

Lewis, Meriwether, and William Clark. The Lewis and Clark Journals (Abridgment) Edited by Gary Moulton, University of Nebraska Press, Lincoln and London, 2003.

Lichatowich, Jim. Salmon, People, and Place. Oregon State University Press, Corvallis, 2013.

Lightfoot, Kent G., and Otis Parrish. California Indians and Their Environment. University of California Press, Berkeley and London, 2009.

Marquez, Joseph Anthony, and Vanessa Anne Marquez. East and West of the Sangre de Cristos, Volume 2: La Familia Marquez. Edited by Vanessa Anne Marquez, JAM Press, Colorado Springs, 1994.

Mathews, Daniel. Natural History of the Pacific Northwest Mountains. Timber Press, Portland, 2017.

Norse, Elliott. Ancient Forests of the Pacific Northwest. Island Press, Washington D.C., and Covelo, CA, 1990.

Pierotti, Raymond. Indigenous Knowledge, Ecology, and Evolutionary Biology. Routledge, London, 2011.

Simmons, Virginia McConnell. The SAN LUIS VALLEY: Land of the Six-Armed Cross, 2nd ed., University Press of Colorado, Niwot, 1994.

STEAMBOAT DAYS on THE RIVER. Oregon Historical Society, Portland, 1969.

Wolf, Edward C., and Seth Zuckerman. SALMON NATION: People, Fish, and Our Common Home. 2nd ed., Ecotrust, Portland, 2003.